MW00745157

ABUSIVE
SUBMISSION

Overcoming Trauma by
the Grace of God

JOY DEIMERT

ABUSIVE SUMBISSION
Copyright © 2018 by Joy Deimert

All rights reserved. Neither this publication nor any part of this publication may be reproduced or transmitted in any form or by any means, electronic or mechanical, including photocopying, recording or any information storage and retrieval system, without permission in writing from the author.

Names and identifying details have been changed to protect the privacy of individuals.

Scripture taken from the HOLY BIBLE, NEW INTERNATIONAL VERSION®. Copyright © 1973, 1978, 1984 International Bible Society. Used by permission of Zondervan. All rights reserved.

Printed in Canada

ISBN: 978-1-4866-1590-2

Word Alive Press
119 De Baets Street Winnipeg, MB R2J 3R9
www.wordalivepress.ca

WORD ALIVE
—P R E S S—

MIX
Paper from
responsible sources
FSC www.fsc.org FSC® C016245

Cataloguing in Publication information may be obtained through Library and Archives Canada.

To my amazing children who had to endure so much.
I love you to the moon and back again!
Thank you to my husband for encouraging me and standing beside me;
for giving me the space I needed to relive and re-grieve.
I love you!

PART I

CHAPTER ONE

ALL I WANTED WAS A BOYFRIEND. ALL I WANTED WAS TO BE LOVED, to be noticed. Was that too much to ask? Oh, I wasn't an ugly duckling, but I certainly wasn't anything like my long, blond-haired, blue-eyed sister who had all the guys phoning and dying to take her out. I was a plain farm girl, who didn't know how to wear makeup and didn't think it would help anyway. I used to look in the mirror and beg God to make my boobs bigger (or at least be able to find them), and to change my looks. Oh, come on gals, as if you've never asked for bigger boobs. And as for praying, yes, I did that a lot and I truly believed God could answer my prayer.

Allow me to tell you a little about myself. I was raised in a small town in the Canadian southern prairies. I went to a small school with two grades to a room and we had to go to a nearby town for grades eleven and twelve.

Going to that new school was overwhelming for me. I had no friends. I didn't fit in. I hated it. I had always struggled with earaches in the younger grades, but in grade eleven it became unbearable. I missed a substantial amount of classes, had surgery and lots of doctor appointments. How I passed I'll never know. My parents felt I wasn't adjusting well either, so they decided to send me to a boarding school for grade twelve a couple hours away from our farm. I had enough credits that I knew I could complete it in one semester—if I would have stayed at home, I wouldn't have been done until June as we didn't have the semester system yet. I did well at this school and was finished in January as anticipated. Then it was on to Bible school in another city six hundred kilometers away for the second semester, and then college for a year the next fall, in the same city.

I did meet one young man in grade twelve and adored him, but for some reason I got scared and broke it off. After that, I couldn't get a guy to look at me. What was wrong with me? I was so lonely and felt like I didn't belong anywhere.

It was only a few weeks prior to graduating from my college program that I started driving around "the block." Lots of people did it. So what? What could it hurt? At least there were occasions when a guy would whistle at me or wave—and yes, I was noticed. Soon it became a habit. On Friday and Saturday nights I couldn't wait to drive around the block—actually about two blocks squared. My window would be open and I would smile as vehicles passed.

Eventually a young man stopped and waved me to stop. I did! Yes, I know how absolutely insane that was, and I know a million bad things could have happened to me, but at that moment I didn't care. We chatted awhile and he asked whether I wanted to go for a drink. There were two other guys in his vehicle. Like a fool, I said yes! We met—me and three total strangers! I don't remember where, but it was in public and I remember my heart beating and thinking that if my mom knew what I was doing, she'd kill me! The driver of the vehicle, Robert, showed interest in me and I soaked up the attention. He asked me out. Wow! I was actually going to have my first date at age eighteen!

It was amazing! Robert had heard the name of my small town. In fact, he had a sister who lived there with her husband. We could talk about so many things and I felt so comfortable with him. During our first few dates we heard about each other's family, how we were brought up, that my sister bought a Volkswagen from him (how coincidental is that?), that his mom lived near my parents, that his dad had passed away at a young age, and that he spent many years in foster homes. I don't know how I never saw or met him earlier while I still lived on the farm.

I finished college and moved back home in search of a job. Robert would drive five hundred kilometers to see me on weekends. My parents weren't too sure of him, but were open-minded to getting to know him, until… My dad had coffee with one of his closest friends in town, and was asked if he knew who I was dating. This friend told my dad that Robert had a bad reputation in town and that he didn't think I should be seeing him. Dad told me he wanted me to stop dating Robert. He gave me no reason. I didn't understand why, and defied Dad's request.

I soon moved off the farm and I moved to the city where I had obtained employment. Robert and I continued to date and he soon moved to his mom's, in the city where I worked, and got a new job. Within a year he proposed and I announced our engagement—which did not go over well with my parents.

You need to understand something. I was raised in a Christian home. My parents influenced me immensely (in a good way), and I wanted to have a marriage and home like theirs. I had a relationship with Jesus. I asked Jesus to come into my life at Bible camp when I was seven, and I always wanted Him as number one in my life. I read my Bible, prayed every day, attended church, attended the same camp until I graduated high school, and attended Bible School. God was first in my life. I had a prayer life that involved morning prayers talking and crying to God. I thanked God many times during the day for preventing me from a possible accident, from swearing, from almost saying something I knew I shouldn't, for helping me hold my temper. I took Him everywhere with me. We talked in the car. We talked on my knees. We talked on walks. We talked while I laid and soaked up the sun. God was my best friend—sometimes I felt He was my only friend!

Robert was not raised in the same home setting. Robert did make a commitment to Jesus while we dated, but looking back, I'm sure he did that for me. He knew I wouldn't marry if it meant being "unequally yoked"—the way I was brought up and taught. After he made his commitment, I felt we were of the same faith and that's all that mattered to give myself permission to marry him. Well, it does take more than being of the same faith (especially if the decision wasn't for the right reason) for a marriage to work, and I was about to find that out. We married shortly before I turned twenty.

We moved four times in the first few years of our marriage and our first baby arrived a little more than two and a half years later. Kevin was a good baby, but I was overwhelmed with being a new mom. I couldn't believe that it "got to me" as much as it did, because I had babysat so much as a teenager, enjoyed every minute of it, and couldn't wait to have my own children. I struggled with the lack of sleep, feeling alone, feeling incompetent, being at home all the time with no parents or family close by, and living on one income.

To add to my stress, when Kevin was only a few weeks old, Robert said something I will never forget. He sat beside me one night while I was nursing Kevin and said he didn't know why, but he got aroused any time he held Kevin.

I was stunned and he caught my reaction. He explained that he was certain it was just thinking of how he loved me and how we made him. I didn't sleep well that night—tossed and turned—and replayed Robert's comment a million times over. I should have acted on it then, but I didn't, and it would come back to haunt me years later.

Somehow, with God's help, I moved forward and learned to enjoy being a stay-at-home mom—cooking and baking with Kevin on the cupboard beside me, allowing Kevin to drop cookies on the cookie sheet, dig his fingers in the bun dough, making homemade playdough in lots of colors so Kevin had something to do when I needed him away from the hot oven, doing yard work while Kevin played in the sandbox, crocheting, sewing outfits for Kevin—sometimes matching with Robert and me, playing the piano, painting the house, going for walks, getting involved at the church, and just enjoying being a new mom enthralled with the adventure of watching each new thing Kevin accomplished and seeing him grow into such a happy little boy.

Not quite two years later, and six weeks early, our second son Logan came along. He was premature—5 pounds, 8 ounces, 17 ¾ inches long. I vividly remember him having trouble breathing and the doctor and nurses working on him. I prayed out loud, "God, please, please don't let him die! Please God, save him!" My doctor was a Christian and he held my hand and was praying too. The ambulance was called to transport the two of us to a more equipped hospital. While everyone's attention was focused on Logan, I became very weak and once we arrived at our destination it became obvious I was going into shock from blood loss.

Logan was whisked into the neonatal intensive care unit while attendants began working on me. I was responding but consistently asking to see my baby. They insisted he was getting the best possible care and that I needed some rest before seeing him. In a few hours a nurse came and wheeled me into NICU, where Logan was hooked up to machines, intravenous, and laying so helpless in an incubator. I could not hold him—only reach my hand through the plastic pockets and hold his tiny fingers.

By the second day, they said I could try nursing him, however his breathing became extremely labored and they took him from me. He had lost weight and was down to four pounds. By the fourth day, I was allowed to try nursing again and this time he latched on with enthusiasm and improvements became noticeable within hours. We were able to take him home within a week. I just knew in my heart that God had something very special planned for Logan. He let him live. Thank you! Thank you!

CHAPTER TWO

WITH THIS NEW LITTLE LIFE CAME MORE CHALLENGING, MORE exhausting years than I could ever imagine! Logan was very sick—all the time—in and out of the hospital to spend time in a croup tent to help him breathe. He coughed and coughed and coughed until he sounded like he was going to pass out. Finally, the doctor suggested we get a croup tent and oxygen pump for his crib at home, in hopes of this cutting down on the hospital stays.

Logan outgrew his cough and soon his unruly temperament became apparent. He would cry and cry endlessly. So much so, I would have to carry him to his room, sit him on the floor and listen to him cry and scream for hours and bang his head against the wall. I would close the door just to get a break from the screaming. On numerous occasions I would ask Logan to put something in the garbage and he would deliberately look at me and put it in the fridge. He seemed so defiant and yet so sweet. How was that possible?

My frustration increased the older he got. When we went to my parents, my dad would tell me we weren't consistent with Logan and that's why he screamed and was so disobedient. I remember once asking Logan to apologize to Grandpa for something mean he had done to him and he deliberately defied me and said, "No." I picked him up and told him he would have a time-out in my parents' room until he came out and said sorry. He sat on the floor and screamed and banged his head on the wall. His eyes became glazed and unfocused. I checked on him every fifteen minutes or so and asked if he had changed his mind and if he would apologize. He stared ahead, screaming and carrying on. This went on for hours. Logan's eyes didn't seem to focus. He was sweating profusely. My dad walked out to do work in the shop because he could not stand it. I explained that we were, in fact, consistent and followed through with discipline but to no avail. Logan screamed for four or five hours, non-stop on most days for no apparent reason. I thought he had a hearing problem but the doctor, health nurse, family—no one believed me.

I would get down to Logan's eye level to talk to him because he seemed like he was in a world of his own and just didn't hear me. I spent hours and hours reading to both Logan and Kevin. I would make Logan look at me and worked so hard to teach him to talk and pronounce words. I would put my finger in his mouth to show him where his tongue should go, in order to pronounce sounds. He did learn to talk—not as clearly as Kevin, though, and I was constantly scolded to not compare children.

It was almost impossible to go anywhere because of Logan's behavior. People stared at us when Logan had a temper tantrum. We used to leave carts full of groceries and just walk out because of the scene Logan was creating. I asked other moms for suggestions, read books and more books, but nothing I tried was working.

By then, I had become pregnant again and a little less than two years after Logan, we had another little boy, Nathan. Thank goodness, Nathan was a happy, contented baby. Kevin loved both of his brothers and was such a little helper. He'd play with Nathan if I needed to attend to Logan or he would try everything in his power to make Logan happy when I needed to nurse Nathan. Kevin would part with his favorite toys just to make either brother happy.

Eventually, social services started contacting us. Someone had reported all the screaming in our home and I told them of our difficulty with Logan. We even had surprise visits and they could see for themselves that he would be sitting in the hall, or his room, and be screaming; sometimes banging his head against the wall—eyes glazed, sweat pouring down his face. I tried hugging, singing, cuddling, restraining, bribery with candy—you name it, I tried it, but with no luck. I prayed and prayed and begged God to help me.

I had people suggest he may be Attention Deficit and had him tested but this was not the case. Finally someone told me they thought Logan was autistic. We contacted the health nurse and our family doctor and asked what we could do. It was suggested that we may need to put Logan in a home—that he would be too much for us to handle. I didn't know how I could possibly do this, but looked into the paperwork and actually began filling it out and considered it. In the meantime, I tried to find a more accurate place to get Logan's hearing tested. I still felt, deep inside of me, this was the true issue, but couldn't get anyone to listen to me.

I finally got an appointment with an audiologist. Guess what? I was told Logan was severe to profoundly deaf in both ears! I was devastated! I was now being told that one of my children, whom I thought was physically perfect, was handicapped and would need lots of special schooling, special training, speech therapy—that he and our whole family would need to learn sign language, that he would need hearing aids, and on and on the list went. I felt like I was living in a nightmare. No, this is not just like wearing glasses—so please don't make light of it. We were soon going to find out how much Logan would be shunned, teased, and how difficult life would be for him.

With this newfound diagnosis came the dilemma of lack of money. Hearing aids were not covered under any provincial medical plan. I wasn't working and we had just moved for the seventh time in our marriage. Robert had another job and money was scarce. Hearing aids were expensive, and to top it all off, we lived in a small community where there was no speech pathologist nearby and no sign-language schools. I contacted different people in the community and asked for some suggestions. I was directed to the school board and told them of our issues with Logan. Logan was three years old and he would need special help at school, too. The school board suggested I contact some service clubs that help handicapped children. We had one club that took a special interest in Logan and funded his hearing aids.

Oh my gosh! You have no idea, absolutely no idea, the change that was about to happen in our home! Shortly after getting the hearing aids, I took Logan and the other two boys to the grocery store. When I opened the cooler door to get milk, Logan started freaking out—nothing unusual for the store patrons, as they had all become accustomed to our disruptions and outbreaks. What do you expect when you have a mother pushing a grocery cart with three little boys aged one, three, and five and pulling another cart with groceries?

However, this time was different. I asked Logan what was wrong. He had quieted down by then. I once again opened the cooler and reached for the milk and Logan started screaming louder than before. Something clicked. In the past few days since Logan had started wearing his hearing aids, I had become strangely sensitive and more aware of hearing things I had previously taken for granted but were perhaps unknown to Logan. I realized the cooler made a loud buzzing when I opened it, but was quiet when closed. Perhaps this unfamiliar sound scared Logan.

I took his hand and helped him pull open the magnetic door and close it, open and close it again. I tried to point out that the noise was strictly from the cooler and there was nothing to fear. He was excited and started playing with the door in amazement as the grin on his face grew larger. A small crowd was forming and a few patrons watched in shock as everyone realized Logan was hearing this for the first time!

Later that same week, I took the boys for a walk. Logan pulled and pulled at my hand as I was pushing Nathan in the baby stroller.

He kept saying, "What's that? What's that?" which, due to his language impairment, sounded more like *wasat wasat!*

I stopped and listened. Logan was hearing a bird—for the first time. The tears were streaming down my cheeks as I bent down to point out the bird in the tree and was overwhelmed with the emotions of sharing this moment, for the first time, with my son. A sadness and an acute awareness of how many times I had punished Logan for disobeying me, overtook me and I wept uncontrollably. In fact, he had probably just never heard me! I was on a sidewalk, in the middle of town, on my knees, hugging all three of my boys and was overwhelmed with the love I had for all three of these precious little ones God gave me, and for the amazing gift of hearing.

The next few months brought about major improvements in our home. Logan was much more contented and quickly becoming accustomed to and dependent on his hearing aids. You should have seen the shock on my parents' face the next time we visited them. My dad could not believe the change in Logan! He could not believe this was the same child! Logan was actually enjoyable to be around and would curl up on Grandpa's knee and laugh and hug him and there were no more screaming spells. I laughed, though. Dad would stand behind Logan and test him and whisper when he wasn't wearing his hearing aids and Logan would still respond. Thus, Dad was skeptical about deafness being the real problem. The family had a lot of learning to acquire about hearing loss and how it wasn't necessarily how loud we spoke—but different pitches, different letters of the alphabet, different sounds—that affected whether Logan could hear.

It didn't take us long to realize that Logan was still going to need speech therapy and would need to attend a special school for the hearing impaired. We moved once again. What's that, the eighth time now in seven years? This time to a bigger center where Logan would be able to get the help he needed. We immediately hooked up with the health unit who made numerous appointments with us: speech pathologist, special school for hearing impaired, handicapped services such as special busing and financing, and a daycare program for handicapped children. Arrangements were made for Logan to attend a special daycare and to be picked up on the handicapped bus.

Things were underway and Logan was changing on a daily basis. It was hard to imagine that he was the same child! In fact, things were progressing so well that we were told they didn't think Logan needed sign language and they thought he could enter a normal school. Wow! Could this really be happening? Yes it could, and Logan entered kindergarten at a public school, at the normal age—three months prior his fifth birthday. They were not going to hold him back, as they thought he would be repeating numerous grades anyway.

Logan adjusted well to his hearing aids. Don't get me wrong. It was a struggle to get him to wear them in the beginning, but once he noticed the advantage, he never took them out. Partway through grade one, the teacher told us Logan was missing a lot in school and she was concerned. I took Logan to see the audiologist again and I was told he would need to wear an amplifying box strapped to his chest and connected to his hearing aids. The teacher would wear a microphone of sorts, which would amplify her voice so Logan could hear everything she said. Logan was teased so much with this, and we begged the audiologist for stronger or better hearing aids. Even with the behind-the-ear hearing aid, Logan was teased. Kids can be so mean.

CHAPTER THREE

SOMEWHERE IN THE MIDDLE OF ALL THIS, I BECAME PREGNANT again. Guess what? Much to my ecstatic surprise, we had a girl. Olivia graced our home when Nathan was two and a half, Logan four—only three months away from entering kindergarten—and Kevin six and almost done kindergarten. By now, all the boys were doing great. Kevin acted the part of big brother and was mommy's major little helper. Logan was well-adjusted and happy, and Nathan was a bubbly, mischievous two-year-old.

Olivia, however, was not a happy baby. She cried constantly. She wouldn't nurse much on one side and her neck was cramped over to the one side all the time. She was slow at everything. She didn't sit until she was ten and a half months old, crawled at eleven months and didn't walk until seventeen and a half months! I went to the doctor constantly with her and tests were done as to why she had no strength in her neck. Olivia had been a difficult delivery and had been turned wrong. They thought she was breach, but turned in the end. Finally had my girl—and she was the slowest at everything! Once she started walking, though, things changed dramatically. She started progressing quickly. It was soon discovered that she was also hearing impaired, however, not as seriously as Logan. Her one ear was moderate to severe and the other was mild to moderate. She soon got hearing aids, but never adjusted to them and would pull them out constantly and refuse to wear them. Because of being able to hear considerably well with her one ear, I was told she wouldn't experience the necessity to wear them like Logan did.

Guess what? Just before Olivia was born, and me about seven months pregnant, we moved again. That's nine times now in eight and a half years. This time we bought a house. I could only hope Robert would settle down to one job and maybe stay in one place for a while. Maybe I could make friends and not have to move away from them. Did I dare to dream this? What about me? What were my emotions, and how was I holding up through these wonderful child-bearing years? I cried lots and lots.

Robert always had excuses to work, or was unemployed and never home, and when he did come home he was too tired to help with the children. Don't get me wrong, he played with them and they loved their daddy. He just didn't do much for them or me. I, on the other hand, baked, sewed matching outfits for all of us, kept a clean house, did laundry, cooked *all* the meals, did all the shopping, did all the budgeting and bill paying, took all the calls from the creditors, dressed the kids, fed the kids, bathed the kids—you name it, I did it. The only problem: I was getting burnt out and extremely frustrated. I was exhausted and desperate to be noticed by someone other than my four little ones. Robert certainly didn't notice me.

The bills were piling up. Robert never bought anything without bringing the loan papers to go with the new purchase. That included gifts to me. Yes, that's right. Even my gifts weren't paid for! The first one was a kitchen center with mixer, blender, etc., and inside one of the bowls was the monthly payment schedule. Or there was the microwave with the monthly payment schedule inside the door, or the VCR, which was really for him because I had no time for television with four little ones—oh, and yes, it also had monthly payments. Yuck! Just buy me a card but forget the stupid payments. Robert would *never* pay cash for anything. Where would he get it? What part of save the cash before you buy didn't he get? I was going insane trying to balance the budget and have enough left over for food. I was beyond frustrated with the creditors chasing us. I didn't want to answer the phone anymore or open the mail. He didn't care. He lived for himself and came home to a comfy home and a family that loved him. What more could he want? I had babysat lots of kids; in fact, I had eight extra ones plus my four, at one time, to bring in extra money. This burnt me out more, but it was the only way to make ends meet. I needed to put food on the table, pay the power bills, and keep the house going—somehow! I also sewed bridesmaid dresses for extra cash.

CHAPTER FOUR

WHEN OLIVIA WAS ABOUT FIVE MONTHS OLD, I STARTED LOOKING for work—something part-time, in the evenings and Saturdays when Robert could be home and we wouldn't need to pay for a sitter. I was still nursing Olivia. None of my kids ever took a bottle. But I really felt I could work around that, if I only worked four hours in the evenings and on Saturdays, I'd have to take a lunch break, so if I could schedule it right, I could still nurse her around my hours. The question of the hour was, who would want someone who hadn't worked for six years and had four kids? I started checking ads in the local paper. I soon applied at a car dealership that needed someone to answer the phone, do paperwork, and do customer satisfaction surveys. The hours were perfect: five till nine in the evenings and nine to five on Saturdays. I went for the interview and was told they had over eighty applicants. Well, I might as well forget it. No one would look at me. However, I had something perhaps no one else had—God. Yes, I prayed lots and asked God to help me find a job. I was shocked to get a call for a second interview and unbelievably was offered the job! We would only need a sitter for an hour or so on weekdays, and then Robert would be home the rest of the time.

Yeah, well, that lasted about a month. Suddenly Robert was avoiding home, working late and even started working Saturdays. I was ticked to say the least! He was in a two-man mechanic shop and he had never worked these hours before. It was obvious the kids were too much for him, and he was avoiding coming home. Good grief, I did everything. What was his problem? The house was spotless, I bathed the kids early so he wouldn't have to, and supper was in the oven every day. There was nothing for him to do but spend a few hours with the kids and put them all to bed at eight and that was a non-issue. All the kids went to bed so easily—put them in their beds and kiss them goodnight. That was it. Was that too much to ask of him, too much to expect of him, while I was out trying to pay for debts he had created? Perhaps this was his way of saying my place was at home. After all, I was making minimum wage minus deductions and now giving more than half my take-home to the sitter. It really didn't make sense, but I didn't care. I had discovered a whole new world out there. Wow! There was more to talk about than poopy diapers, sick babies, soap operas, and kids fighting.

I worked with mostly male employees. I was being noticed and appreciated for my efficiency, for my friendliness, for my baking which I took to work quite often, and for just being me. Hey, look at me! There's more to me than just being a mom. Look at me! I exist! I count! I really matter in this life! With this newfound recognition, I began to thrive and go above and beyond to be noticed. I got away from the phone and typing and started showing vehicles as customers came in, and because I typed the spec sheets, I knew lots about the size of engines, whether they had extras and what those extras were. Soon my boss recognized what I was doing and told me I should consider selling instead of being taken advantage of and doing the work while the men were being paid for it. I laughed, but he was serious. There were no female car salespeople in our community that I knew of. Could I do this?

In the meantime, things were deteriorating at home. Robert was home less and less, and I was still doing everything I had done prior to working, but now I had added my job of twenty-seven hours a week. Then, one day while I was baking and getting supper ready in the kitchen, I heard Kevin and Logan giggling downstairs. I listened for a while and enjoyed hearing their laughter while the other two little ones were napping. I snuck downstairs to peak around the corner to see what they were up to and to tell them not to be too noisy so the other two wouldn't be woken. I stopped in my tracks and was devastated and shocked to death to see what was before me! They were performing oral sex on each other! They were six and four. Where on earth would they ever have learned anything like this? This was *not* normal boys playing. This was *not* normal behavior. I flipped out and started screaming and told them to stop right now. They immediately obeyed, but had no idea why I was so upset. It was like this definitely wasn't the first time and they had absolutely no shame and no clue what they had done wrong! I sent them to their rooms and was just shaking. I needed to calm down and think. *Think, Joy. Think.*

I know I was extremely naïve. My parents never talked about sex and I knew nothing when I got married, but I was pretty confident this behavior would have to be shown and was not a natural thing. I just didn't know who to talk to or where to turn first. I had to be at work in a few hours. How was I going to leave? What if the sitter was showing and encouraging this? What if my sons had been abused? What if—a million what ifs? I made a phone call to a Children's Hospital and asked to talk to someone involved with sexual abuse. Of course, they weren't accepting phone calls without appointments. However, I explained to the receptionist what had just happened and whether she thought I needed help. She told me I was blowing it out of proportion and that I should calm down and this was normal inquisitiveness for young boys, that I just needed to teach them it was inappropriate. I tried to calm down, but was shocked at her response.

I called Robert at work and told him and he got upset with me— yes, with me. He told me to grow up and read some books on raising boys. Okay, get a grip Joy. You're being told that it's normal so there's nothing to worry about, right? Right? Needless to say, my mind was not on work that night and it was extremely hard to joke with the guys I worked with, and to concentrate on anything. This was *not* something that I could discuss with them either.

I was so nervous around my boys. What should I say to them? Should I say Mommy was wrong to holler and that I was sorry but I didn't want them to do that again? I finally got the nerve to call my sister and sister-in-law to get their opinions and they were both appalled also. They both agreed the boys must have been shown this and it was not normal. They both had boys and had nothing like this happen in their homes.

I knew if I made too big of a deal with this, the boys would clam up and perhaps have inhibitions towards sex later in life. So I finally sat down with them and told them they should never let anyone touch their privates. No one, absolutely no one, and if someone did, they should tell me immediately. I told them that when they were older, they could ask me questions about their privates and I would always be there to answer their questions. They both kind of laughed and went off to play, seemingly unaffected by the whole situation.

I was contemplating quitting my job. I was nervous now about outsiders being in our home. I was questioning everything the sitters said and did. Maybe I shouldn't be working. I begged Robert to change his hours and told him he was the one who should have been home with the kids and we shouldn't need sitters. I told him he needed to be a part of their lives, too, and this shouldn't all be on my shoulders. It wasn't fair. He disagreed and said I should quit my job if I didn't like the way the sitters handled our kids. He told me I was over-protective and needed to lighten up.

CHAPTER FIVE

ONE EVENING WE WERE OVER AT FRIENDS FOR ROBERT'S BIRTHDAY, playing cards. I had all four kids in their pajamas and sleeping on the friend's bedroom floor. We did this a lot. The kids went to bed so easily and we would play cards till late and load the kids in the car and take them home into their own beds and they wouldn't even awaken! I was not a drinker, and I only saw Robert take an occasional drink. However, on this particular night, Robert was having one drink after the other and he was getting drunk. I told him it was time to leave and he staggered towards me and seemed upset about the suggestion of leaving. I warmed up the car and started carrying the kids out one by one.

I asked him if he was coming with us and he said, "No, none of us are leaving. We are staying longer."

I told him he could stay but the kids were in the car and we were going home. I went out to the car and was pulling away when suddenly Robert was attempting to jump in the passenger door. He was leaning through the door and reached across where Nathan was sitting and had his elbow pinned under Nathan's throat and Nathan was screaming and screaming until he passed out!

Kevin was hollering in the backseat, "Stop, Daddy! Leave him alone. He's dead! He's dead! Stop! Daddy, Stop!"

I was hysterical as Robert was trying to throw the car into park. He reached for the keys and broke the keychain. Finally someone from the house came out and pulled Robert out of the car, onto the street, and hollered at me, "Get out of here. Leave! Hurry up and leave!" I checked my rearview mirror as I spun away and saw Robert lying on the street and wondered if he was okay but sped ahead as Nathan regained consciousness, screaming and crying. Thank goodness! All I cared about was getting the kids to the safety of their own beds and then would try to make sense of what just happened.

The next morning the kids asked where Daddy was. I explained that he stayed at our friend's home for the night. They said they didn't want him home. They said they were scared and asked why Daddy tried to kill Nathan. Within hours, Robert came home and the kids ran to their rooms. As he stood at the door, he apologized and said he didn't know what came over him and promised it would never happen again. The kids didn't come out of their rooms for hours and when they did, he hugged each of them and told them how sorry he was.

Nathan kept asking, "Why, Daddy? Why do you want me dead?"

Kevin was angry, very angry, and wouldn't talk to Robert at all.

A few days later, I was doing laundry and had stripped Kevin's bed. When I was remaking it, I lifted the mattress to push the blankets under and I felt something. I reached under and there was a wooden bat. I called Kevin and asked why this was under his mattress. Kevin hollered to leave it there. He explained that he needed it in case Daddy hurt us again and he would have to break a window or something to rescue the family. Kevin cried and cried and said he couldn't sleep. He said he was trying to figure out how he'd get out of the basement and get to the top level in our small bi-level home in order to rescue the other two boys and Olivia. He didn't know how he'd ever get them out of the windows without hurting them. He thought it was too high and he couldn't find any ladders. He was petrified Olivia would break her neck if he had to drop her to the ground from her window.

I bent down and hugged Kevin and pulled him onto my lap. I reassured him he wouldn't have to rescue them. I told him I would be the one protecting them and he didn't need to worry. I told him I would put the bat under his mattress so he would feel safe. I stopped and prayed and asked Jesus to protect my four precious children and begged God to not allow Daddy to be angry at us anymore. Kevin's tears and fear cut me like a knife. His fear was so very real!

Then the nightmares began—Nathan's, I mean. He would wake up screaming and screaming. I would go to his room and he would be shaking and screaming that there was a monster in his bed and he wouldn't quit touching him. I would calm him down and he'd fall back to sleep. I supervised every television program the boys were watching so there wasn't anything scary and told the sitters they couldn't watch TV at all if I wasn't home. The days following his outbursts, I would question Nathan about his dreams and ask if he remembered anything. Eventually he told me he was scared and that there was a monster coming into his room, making him do things he didn't like, hurting him, and the monster slept with mommy but the monster wasn't daddy. He didn't know who he was. I discussed his nightmares with Robert, asking him what his thoughts were on it, and he sloughed it off on kid's imaginations and was not concerned in the least.

Other things started happening too. Robert wasn't sleeping well. He was suddenly getting up in the middle of the nights and wandering around the house. He started having headaches—severe ones. He would sweat over one side of his face and his one eye would become glazed. We made many trips to emergency and he got shots of morphine to control them. Eventually he was diagnosed with cluster headaches. Some nights he would sit up in bed and start hollering at me, swearing and calling me every abusive name under the sun. I would cower and curl up, scared he was going to hit me, and yet sometimes wishing he would, just so I would have proof of how bad things were becoming. Proof of why I had to leave. He'd often get out of bed and shake his finger at me and threaten to take my life. Then just as suddenly as the outbursts began, he'd crawl back into bed and fall into a deep sleep. Soon this escalated into him talking to an invisible person. He would holler at this person and tell them to get out of our room and leave me alone. Then he'd be the other person and say he could do whatever he wanted. The following mornings I would discuss it with him and he wouldn't remember. I didn't believe him. That was an excuse, as far as I was concerned, for saying whatever he wanted. I told Robert I thought he needed to see a doctor, that he was becoming two people I didn't know and didn't like. The kids were being woken by these outbursts and I could hear them whimpering in their rooms, but I was too scared to move.

Robert began criticizing the way I dressed. He had never noticed me at all for nine years and now he was complaining. He walked in our room one day as I was getting ready for work. I was going to wear a sweater dress, and in order to prevent the lines showing under my dress, I quite often wore the all-in-one pantyhose. He flipped out and said I was a slut and that he now knew why I was going to work. Unbelievable! I had worn these pantyhose for years and years under slacks or dresses to church and other places, and he never noticed because I don't think he ever saw me get dressed or undressed before! Married for nine years and never naked in front of each other? Is this possible? Quit laughing! This is not a laughing matter. It seemed he was never around when I was getting ready, and it was made clear that I always had to wear a nightie to bed and the lights were out whenever we made love. How could I help but wonder how disgusting I must be? How revolting and ugly! So much so that Robert couldn't even look at me.

Oh, speaking of making love, that was very different also. Remember I told you that I was quite naïve and was brought up with no knowledge of sex or relationships? Robert was my first. I didn't know what was appropriate or normal. I didn't know what to expect or to look forward to. I didn't know what I was supposed to do to entice my husband to notice me. What can I say? Robert had difficulty performing. I didn't know that was unusual. I just thought I was doing something wrong, that I wasn't pretty enough or my boobs were too small (there I go again). I don't think he ever touched them in all the years we were married—and you wonder why I'm so hung up on that issue.

Amazingly, though, it seemed that if one of the kids slept in our room, like when they were newborns, or when we went away and they slept on the floor, those were the nights he wanted to make out. I remember being frustrated and angry because those were the nights I didn't want any part of it. Now that I look back, I wonder how I got pregnant four times! I remember reading a book about romancing your spouse and deciding I would try something. Robert was showering and the kids were all in bed. I lit some candles in our room, disrobed, and went to join him in the shower. I opened the bathroom door and as I pulled back the shower curtain to step in, Robert exploded. He grabbed the curtain to cover himself and swore at me and hollered, "Get out now!" When he came into the bedroom where I was once again in my nightie and hiding tightly under the covers in bed, he told me I was a whore and that he didn't know me, I disgusted him, and he was sick of me!

Chapter Six

ALL OF THIS FINALLY LED ME TO TAKE ALL FOUR KIDS AND ME TO the women's shelter to find refuge. The kids were one, three, five, and seven. I was a mess, an absolute mess. I didn't know if I needed to face reality that Robert was the abuser—that he was sexually touching our children, or whether I was the one who needed help in learning how to cope with life in general. I phoned my boss and told him I'd have to miss a couple days of work, and because I had never missed before, he was concerned and asked what was going on. I opened up and told him I was at the shelter. He told me to take care of myself and not worry about my job, that it would be there waiting for me and if I needed anything, anything at all, to call him. I stayed at the shelter for several days and finally got the courage to phone Robert and tell him I was coming home but that he was going to have to move out. I was unbelievably nervous when I came home. Robert wanted to talk it out and I said he still needed to move. He had a sister living in town and he could move in with her for the first while.

Robert came back later with a friend for some furniture. He began to load things we had agreed on. Suddenly he started swearing and hollering at me when he was taking things from the bedroom. He shoved me down on the bed and picked up one of the nightstands and had it over his head ready to clobber me with it. I hadn't realized Kevin was there and he suddenly started screaming and begging Daddy not to kill Mommy! The friend ran into the room and grabbed Robert and the nightstand and set it down.

This was the start of the most dreadful years of my life. Counseling, accusations, sleepless nights, and changing the locks and adding dead-bolts was only the beginning. I sought out friends, Christian counselors, social services, doctors, and family. Robert was bitter and angry and wanted to come home. Get this: he actually told me he thought I should have an affair because I would realize how good I had it! Are you kidding me? He also told me it was a time for confessions, and because of things he had done, he thought I should be tested for AIDS! How many girls had he slept with? What on earth was he trying to tell me?

Robert didn't take the children out for five months. Suddenly, he wanted to take them for a weekend and I was truly scared to allow it. He told me I was losing it and needed help. Why on earth wouldn't they be safe with their own dad? I went back to social services and said we needed help. I wanted them to question the children and find out what was going on—to see if professionals could get some answers, because I was desperate to find the truth. Robert was going to my siblings and to my parents to tell them *I* was the one who needed psychological help. I felt very alone. What if my parents believed him and not me? Was I going insane? Was any of this reality or were the past events all a nightmare? Was I making more of this than it was, or should I forget everyone else and go with my gut instincts and protect my children? How do I do this when no one will believe me or listen? I prayed. Oh, I prayed! I know you're probably saying, how can there be a God in all of this? But God was the only one I could count on. He was the only one who would listen when I cried out. This didn't pull me away from God; it only drew me closer to Him. I grabbed my Bible and desperately searched for verses of reassurance. *"I can do everything through Him who gives me strength"* (Philippians 4:13). *"And my God will meet all your needs according to his glorious riches in Christ Jesus"* (Philippians 4:19). Oh Lord, give me strength!

I would wake up and pray for hours and hours for some kind of direction to whom I could go to for help. I went to numerous Christian counselors to explain the situation and ask for advice. Over and over I was told divorce was wrong—absolutely wrong. I had no support whatsoever. I felt like no one believed me. I couldn't prove any of my suspicions. I was told the only grounds for leaving, if absolutely necessary, was adultery—and that wasn't an issue I could prove other than him telling me to be tested for AIDS.

Robert finally got a court order granting him reasonable access to see the children. I had *no* rights to withhold them. He was also supposed to pay fifty dollars per month, per child. He made arrangements to pick up the children and I was sick—just sick. How do I hand over my precious little children to someone I think is sexually abusing them? How do I do that? I had no proof. I only had circumstantial evidence and a knot in my stomach that almost made me puke when I thought about it. Robert had no clue how to handle four kids for a whole weekend. He was in a basement suite with no extra beds, no toys, and not much food.

The children were returned on Sunday evening; late, filthy clothes (even though I sent lots), hungry, dirty faces and hands, and crying. So I had to get all four bathed, fed, and off to bed knowing the next morning would be a challenge because they'd had no afternoon naps and it was already way past their bedtime. Olivia screamed when I put her into the tub—just screamed. Her privates were so red and irritated, and not just from a wet diaper, in my opinion. She had rashes before and never screamed before like this when she went into the tub—she loved baths. The next day I asked them if they had fun at Daddy's and asked what they did, where they slept, and was Olivia crying lots. They said they played lots but missed their own beds and toys. I spoke to the police and to Social Services again. I wanted someone to believe me—that he shouldn't have time alone with the children. Robert was telling people he thought he was two people. He described, to others, that he was getting so frustrated and angry he thought about hiring someone to kill me.

Finally another court date was set to dispute access. Robert was questioned extensively at this Preliminary Inquiry. Robert was under oath and said he often wondered what it would be like to hang the children out the car window and watch the children's heads bounce off the highway as he was travelling sixty miles per hour, or what it would be like to throw them out the window. Robert explained that once he talked about it, it was no longer a threat. He was asked about the time he choked Nathan and why he couldn't stop himself that time. He didn't deny the incident and said he knew it would never happen again. He was asked how often he thought about killing me. He didn't deny that either, and said that when he thinks about killing me he stays away then. He said he has also talked to others about committing suicide. He said that when he feels bad thoughts or feels like two people, he just stays away from the family or talks it out until the feelings go away. After all this, he was still given reasonable access—not supervised. What is wrong with the judicial system? Could they not hear for themselves how dangerous and unstable he was?

At the same time, the prior arrears for child support were wiped out entirely. However, they were increased from fifty to one hundred dollars per child, per month. Whoopee! Let's erase the prior debt and increase the amount, and honestly think he'll pay anything? If he couldn't or wouldn't pay two hundred a month, why would he begin paying four hundred? What a joke!

Of course, through all of this, I was still trying to compose myself enough to hold a full-time job—a new one, which required lots of studying and taking exams. I would study after the children went to bed and then get up at 4 AM. I needed to miss days for court, involve the children in soccer, church drama and choir, school activities and, to top it all off, deal with the divorce and mounting debt.

I thought I was smart. I cut up credit cards—mine and snuck his before I asked him to leave, switched the phone and utilities into my name, and started my own bank account and took my name off our joint one. However, it didn't take me long to realize how stupid I really was. Stupid! Stupid! Stupid! Just cutting up the credit cards didn't really mean anything. Robert just called and said he lost them and got new ones. The big catch was that when he got these new cards, I was still listed as a co-applicant, and thus, responsible for the debt. Of course he started racking up more bills and more debt for me. He quit making payments on any other bills we had. He never paid the mortgage. He never paid a dime towards child support. I went to the bank and creditors to take my name off the accounts; however, they wouldn't allow me to do that without bringing the balance to nil.

I had no money. I was only making $1,200 gross a month. My take-home was around $900. The mortgage was $550. That left $350 for food, utilities, daycare for two and afterschool care for the other two, lawyer bills, gas, and on and on. I applied for welfare to help subsidize me. I had medical bills, hearing aid bills, dental bills, clothes for growing children, and an old wreck of a car needing constant repairs. Thank goodness I had the Lord. I never would have made it. There were days I wondered what we would eat. *"For He will deliver the needy who cry out, the afflicted who have no one to help"* (Psalm 72:12). I soon found out the children loved macaroni for breakfast or cereal for supper. We managed; somehow we managed and I always made it a fun time. I never let on to the children that we were poor and how difficult things were for me. This was *not* their problem. It was mine and we would survive. I knew we would survive, with the help of God. I was brought up with tithing to the Lord—giving ten percent. I remember vividly my dad teaching that God should be first, not last. Dad said if we would give God first place, He would always take care of us and supply our needs. Not our wants, but our needs! So off the meager $900 I made, I gave $90 to the church. We never went hungry and we always had a roof over our heads!

CHAPTER SEVEN

ONE AND A HALF YEARS AFTER OUR SEPARATION, I GOT A CALL from the daycare. Nathan had spoken to one of the workers and told them Daddy had a secret—that "Daddy touches Logan in his privates." I approached the children about Dad's secrets, but they wouldn't tell me anything. However, later that evening, Kevin called Robert and said Mom knows about the secrets. A friend of mine picked up one of the other phones and was listening in to the conversation. Robert asked which secrets Mom knew. Kevin told him the one about touching Logan's privates. Then Robert asked if Mom knew any of the other secrets. Kevin told him, "No, and we won't tell, Dad."

I brought these allegations to my lawyer's attention. He immediately attended court to get an order directing no access at all to Robert until a court date a couple weeks later. On that court date, the judge granted supervised access until an investigation could be conducted by Social Services. I actually thought I was finally getting somewhere. However, everything was about to blow up in my face!

Robert agreed to a lie detector test at the police station. He failed it. He told the sergeant that he probably failed it because he still gets an erection while holding Olivia. I wasn't given any further details in regards to the test and was told this wasn't admissible in court but it aroused suspicions worth investigating further.

The boys went to counseling and revealed it was Dad who asked them to "suck on each other's pee-pees." They told the counsellor they were often in the bedroom alone with him at his house just hugging and kissing, however, not the same way they kiss Mom. Logan was asked if he could say "No" to Dad and he said he couldn't say no because, "Dad was always on top."

Olivia was trying to kiss me at home and was trying to put her tongue in my mouth. I shoved her away and told her to smarten up and that wasn't nice. She explained that she did it with Daddy all the time. When she was questioned by a male Social Worker, she got very upset and threw up all over him.

While the boys were being questioned, one of them was listing numerous things he remembered Daddy doing to him and suddenly said, "I can't remember the next point that Mommy told me." Well that ended that, and I was accused of prompting and coercing the children. I know I was panicked and I would sit and have the children go over and over what they told me Daddy did to them and would say, "Okay, that's three things, don't forget that." Oh how I wished the police and Social Services would have acted sooner and would have warned me not to talk to the children at all. There was way too much time between me reporting what happened to the police and then waiting for them to interview the children. No one else seemed concerned or worried except for me. It was crazy. It was like they still wanted me to hand over my children and not care about what would happen to them.

I would go to the pastor, friends, and family and they would look at me as if I was the liar and making this all up. Robert was going to see *my* parents and family and telling them I desperately needed help. I felt like they were taking his side and it was easier for them to believe I was psycho than him a pedophile. I know it was hard to believe any parent could touch their child sexually. I know that…but come on, I was flesh and blood. Why would they believe him before me? Part of me began to feel the whole world was against me—that no one believed me, that I'd have to keep handing my children over to their abuser and let it happen. I would attend church every Sunday with four little ones. No one ever offered to sit and help me. No one ever asked us out for meals. No one ever asked how we were doing. If I had to take one to the bathroom, I'd have to take all four because I didn't dare leave three left unattended during the service.

But…I kept going, searching for answers, hoping I'd find just one person who would acknowledge what I was saying and make me feel like I wasn't going crazy! I believed God would get me through this. Sometimes I felt Christians were my worst enemies, judging me more than anyone else. No one even asked to hear my story. They just saw me as a single woman coming to church alone with four little ones. No one had to tell me divorce was wrong. I knew that. But did God expect me to stay under those circumstances? My faith in God was so strong that it didn't matter who believed me and how alone I was. I was never going to turn my back on God. Never! Was Satan trying to get me? Well, that was never going to happen!

CHAPTER EIGHT

ROBERT GOT A COURT ORDER, AGAIN, ALLOWING REGULAR ACCESS every second weekend. The judge refused to hear about Robert failing the lie detector test. The judge said he was sick of this matter being brought to court and was convinced I would do anything to prevent Robert from access. The judge said he wanted this issue brought to a conclusion immediately and never wanted to see it in court again!

When Robert came to pick up the children the next weekend, Olivia was screaming and had to have her fingers peeled off my neck in order to give her to Robert. When she was put in the truck she was screaming and screaming out the window, "Mommy, Mommy, nooooooo..." He left the children alone while he went to help someone move. The children were about nine, seven, five, and three. While the children were playing alone outside, Logan fell in a big hole. He got hung by his arm catching on a steel peg protruding from a cement wall (I assumed it was construction of a basement or something). Logan was screaming and screaming. Someone from inside the apartment came running out and searched for Robert. I don't know if Kevin rescued him or what the details were. However, Kevin said it took forever for Dad to come and take Logan to the hospital for fourteen stitches!

Right after this, Kevin started getting up in the middle of the night and coming to my room. I asked what was wrong and he said Dad told him he wanted to know who Mom was sleeping with and that he was supposed to check and report back. Kevin snuck into my room for weeks and would cry and tell me how tired he was and that he couldn't get up anymore. It didn't matter how many times I tried to reassure him that Mom had no one in her room, he still kept getting up.

I got a phone call from my lawyer. Robert was taking me to court for specified access. He wanted to take the children to BC, the day after the court date, for two weeks. He was planning to take his mom with him. He also requested the children every second weekend after he returned. He won! My gosh, he won again! I had one night to pack and get the children ready to hand over to a man I believed was abusing them! I wondered if I was handing the children over for the last time—that I may never see them again! I taught Kevin that night how to phone me collect from a payphone. I told him to call as often as he wanted. I held on to my children so tightly and cried and cried as I kissed them goodbye.

Kevin called—crying, homesick, scared—and said he didn't think they were ever coming home again. He said he was bored and they were sleeping in the truck. He said they were taught that when there was a Stop sign it meant, "Stop, Take, Off, Pants." Kevin called me several times begging me to come and find him. He said that while Dad was filling with gas, he would say he was going to the washroom but would go to the payphone instead and call me. My lawyer told me there was nothing I could do. We didn't have proof of anything and my hands were tied.

The children did come home to me. Praise the Lord! What a relief!

Numerous people, including my brother and his wife, told me Robert told them explicitly how he was planning to kill me. He described cutting me up and hanging me by pieces in my own basement and wondering who would find me first.

I began contemplating and searching into running away and hiding. I actually found someone who would help me. There was an underground system that would assist me. All I'd have to do is leave—no goodbyes, no clothes, no personal belongings, no warnings to anyone. Just go. It was set up so that the children and I would spend one night at an undisclosed place. They would feed me and give enough money and directions to my next location. This would be my life for the next several weeks until I reached an unknown destination where I would be set up with a place to live, a job, a new identity, schools for the children, etc. The biggest catch was that I would *never* be able to contact any family, and I mean no one ever.

I struggled with this so much. My parents were in their seventies and my mom had just been in the hospital with medical issues. I loved them dearly. What about my brothers and sisters whom I adored? What a huge decision! Yes, my children were more important to rescue than any of this other stuff, but I was scared. Scared to be alone forever, scared of the unknown, of having no family support, of what the children would think. And above all else, I was scared of being caught and prosecuted and then Robert getting full custody. Oh I prayed and prayed and prayed, "God, help me. Please God, help me!"

Olivia told one of my girlfriends that Daddy has a black dress, and high black shoes like Mommy's. She said that Daddy tickles her—and he doesn't stop. She said he tickles her bum and her face is in the pillow and she keeps telling him to stop and he won't and it hurts so badly!

The next day on the way to daycare, Olivia said, "Mommy, don't ever let Daddy get mad at you. Daddy gets mad at me. Do you know what he does, when he gets mad at me? He puts his gun in my pee-pee and it hurts real badly. If Daddy gets mad at you, he'll put the gun in your pee-pee and I don't want you to get hurt, Mommy."

I tried to reassure her. What could I say? I made arrangements to see a pediatrician. Everything appeared to be fine. Of course, Social Services were notified again and marked our file "High Risk." Arrangements were made for her to be videoed at the police station. It was a disaster. She threw up again. We tried again a few days later and the only thing she said was that Daddy has a black dress and a gun but he put it away now.

There were a number of letters back and forth between our lawyers discussing the divorce, property division, child support, and access. Christmas was coming and Robert would be getting them this year. I was beside myself. What was Christmas without my kids? I decorated the house, put up a tree, bought presents, and tried to make it a happy time. I told the children they would be with Daddy and could look forward to coming home to open their presents. I debated about letting them open them ahead and take some with them; however, on prior occasions when they took toys, they were not returned.

They left for six days. Kevin called several times, crying and upset. Robert was in a basement suite. He had no tree, no turkey, and no presents. I kept reassuring Kevin that we would pretend it was Christmas all over again when he'd come home. I spent my first Christmas alone. I had a few invitations for Christmas dinner, but I wasn't going to leave the house in case the children phoned. I thought I was strong enough and it was no big deal—after all, we'd celebrate later. However, when Christmas Day arrived, I spent most of it crying and crying. I went to each of the children's beds and hugged their pillows and prayed for each one. I did get a phone call and got to talk to all four, and they told me they were having soup for supper. I begged God to take care of them and that nothing evil would happen to them. I finally drifted off to sleep on one of their beds; and thus survived my first Christmas alone.

A few weeks later, Robert took the children for a weekend again. The children told me Robert drove them in his truck onto the partially frozen river by the power house. The truck broke through the ice and both passenger wheels were in the water. Olivia smashed her head on the windshield. All the children had severe nightmares about drowning for weeks after. Seriously, what was wrong with this man? Why would he put his children's lives at risk?

In the meantime, someone told me about a program in Canada called "Victims of Violence". I found out their address and sent them a letter explaining my dilemma: my suspicions of the sexual abuse, no one believing me, the questioning of the children getting nowhere, and Robert's failed polygraph test. I got a response and was asked for the Social Worker and the detective's names and addresses. I supplied this information. I never heard anything from them again. I contacted them again but never got any results.

CHAPTER NINE

THE DIVORCE WAS FINALLY SETTLED, THREE YEARS AFTER WE SPLIT up. I was given full custody with Robert getting reasonable access and three weeks in August and alternating Christmases. The child support payments were increased to $150/month per child for a total of $600/month. Of course, once again, very little was paid from the prior order. Then there was a seizure of Robert's truck and tools. He objected, claiming they were exempt because they were for work, so the items were released. Robert appealed the divorce on the 30th and final day he could. However, he withdrew the appeal four or five months later and it was finalized.

I asked my dad how much money we owed him. I know we had gotten $5,000 for the down payment on the house, and I knew I had asked him a couple other times for some money. Dad sat down and wrote me a letter, listing what he'd given us. I was shocked, absolutely shocked! Robert must have phoned him for money without my knowledge. I believed this should be part of our matrimonial debt, however Robert adamantly disagreed. He said it was a gift and no way was he going to pay him back!

So now came the big decision. I would have to sell the house. I knew rent would be just as much as the mortgage payment, but I just had too much debt and had to pay my lawyer. I had already paid almost $3,400 towards debts Robert had incurred: Sears, Canadian Tire, Superior Propane, Revelstoke, bank overdraft, his first bounced mortgage payments, his truck insurance, his truck payments, and over $4,000 in mortgage payments. I listed the house, after a lot of confrontation from Robert. I didn't know until the house sold, and the profit was being divided, that Robert had racked up more unpaid debts and these debtors had placed liens on the house—his lawyer, his vehicle loan, and numerous others. I was devastated. I thought the profit would be split in half. It was not! His debts all got paid, and then the balance still got divided, leaving me some to give my dad and not the other debts at all. Robert did not give me a dime from his profit.

Oh, I almost forgot. Guess where Robert's half of the leftover profit went? It paid his court costs of $1,273.17 and the arrears of $2,526.77 to *my* child support. Yes, I basically paid my own child support from all the payments I made on our mortgage. How ironic! All the credit cards, outstanding home bills, loans, and balances on all the other bills all became mine in order to get them cancelled and get my name off completely. This was so unfair. I was taken to court for several of these, and the judge took pity on me and demanded the interest stop, as of that date. I did not have the option of declaring bankruptcy. The new job I had with finance and insurance would not allow me to work there if I had. Now that I was declaring single on income tax and due to my low income, there was a substantial yearly tax credit per child. Within two years I had all my/our debts paid. Please note that because I was a recipient of welfare, I had to submit these tax credits to my lawyer. The lawyer would then make payments toward the matrimonial debt and would also have to submit an affidavit signed by me stating the money was not used for personal use or for the children. Of course, being forced to go to a lawyer for this incurred more legal costs for me.

Robert's visits were sporadic. He was not complying with the divorce order. He would scare the children by saying he would probably never see them again. He would drop them off at church with dirty faces and dirty clothes. Olivia complained of a sore tummy and would scream when she was bathed and complained that her "bum was sore because Daddy touched it."

Olivia was questioned once again by a female police officer and disclosed a few sexual things Daddy did to her. Kevin was talking about suicide. He felt he had no reason to live. He knew Daddy didn't love him anymore, and told how Daddy would pull him by his ears and throw him onto a bed. Kevin said Dad spanked and hit him repeatedly and often dragged him by his hair. Kevin said he knew he wasn't strong enough to "beat up Daddy." Kevin was showing aggression in school and was in danger of being expelled. He was refusing to go with Robert now completely. Nathan started having stress-related problems. He was having severe nightmares and would wake up screaming, saying he couldn't breathe and questioning whether Daddy would ever choke him again. Nathan's eyes started blinking uncontrollably and he couldn't stop it. When I took him to a doctor, I was told this was totally stress-related.

Olivia was again invited to the police station to be videoed with the female officer. Olivia was much more relaxed and open with her as opposed to being alone with a man. The police officer had anatomical dolls. Olivia pointed out and named body parts. The man's penis was a gun. I had always thought the gun was an object Robert was using, but never once put two and two together that it was his penis. The girl's vagina was her pee-pee. Olivia said she hated it when Daddy shot her. She said she didn't like getting wet and cried when Daddy got her tummy all wet. She also said she hated putting the gun in her mouth and how she thought she was choking. She said she hated the taste when Daddy shot the gun. Then the officer asked her how she would sit with Daddy. Olivia lay on her back on the couch and pulled both her legs up on either side of her cheeks, by her ears, and held them and said Daddy would then kneel in front of her between her legs.

CHAPTER TEN

I FILED FOR AN INTERIM VARIATION TO THE DIVORCE ORDER
with the above details listed in an affidavit. The judge dismissed my
application, but insisted there be a trial regarding the issues of custody
and access. I had no money, no moral support, and was feeling frustrated,
scared, and very alone. I was on legal assistance and now that lawyer
said he could not handle this. He suggested I apply to have an Amicus
Curiae appointed by the court. He explained that the Amicus provides
independent legal representation for children in cases where custody
and access are the major issues. This would be beneficial because the
children would have their own legal counsel (that I didn't need to pay
for) and would benefit from the marshalling or expert evidence such as
psychologists' reports, which would assist the court in arriving at the
ultimate decision. Social Services was contacted and finally they went to
court for the children and asked for supervised access for Robert until
the trial. There were numerous motions set forth to the court, with the
final one resulting in interim supervised access to Robert and a trial date
finally set.

A new lawyer was assigned to represent the children. He arranged
for a psychologist in a larger city to meet with all of us, at government
expense. I had to miss a week of work. I took a babysitter with me
and we were given a hotel room. Appointments were made for each of
the children individually, for me alone, for me with the children, for
Robert alone, and then for Robert with the children. The babysitter was
wonderful and stayed with the other children while I took each to see

the psychologist. The psychologist wrote a 21-page report which was submitted to the children's lawyer, my lawyer, and Robert's lawyer.

I also received a call from the police station just before I left for the city and was asked to pick up a package that was to be given to the psychologist. There was a cassette tape and a video tape. The cassette ended up being a copy of Robert's polygraph test. In the psychologist's report, she stated that on the cassette Robert did say that Olivia was sleeping on his chest and was almost choking him so he "slid her down" and "that's when (he) got the erection." Robert indicated that his shorts were on but "down." Robert confirmed that his penis was near Olivia's rear end. He then stated, "I tried to get to feel how a child molester would feel like," "I feel totally disgusted," and "I'll still go for help because that's a sign I need help...but I don't want to be charged, that's the thing." On the tape, Robert stated, "In my mind I never did anything to Logan." He later indicated that he never did anything "intentionally" to any of the boys. He stated that he knew he had a problem and wondered if it was treatable. When Robert was encouraged to discuss the matter with the polygraph operator, Robert indicated he was afraid to tell anything about Olivia because "that's a dark secret that I'd just as soon forget." Robert later told the polygraph operator that after telling him about Olivia, he was "relieved."

According to the psychologist's report, the video was of Olivia talking to the female police officer. I was glad the psychologist got to see and hear Olivia disclosing those details. I was hoping that these two things, plus the interviews with our family, would present a good overview for the psychologist to make a professional conclusion.

Do you have any idea how unnerving it was for me to be tested and examined to see if *I* was fit to have custody of my own children? What if I lost my children after all this? What if she found me incapable of raising them, or worse yet, what if she found nothing wrong in what Robert was allegedly doing to the children? I was basically putting myself into the hands of the kids' lawyer and the psychologist. My future with my kids was on the line. What if I had messed up by putting my kids into the hands of the government?

I also found out from the psychologist's report that Robert submitted an audiotape from a private investigator Robert had hired to interview the children. The psychologist stated in her report, "*It was difficult to evaluate, due to the number of stops and starts on it. The private investigator asked some questions which were quite leading.*"

I knew I was being followed and watched, but I didn't know by whom, or who hired this person, until I read an article in the local newspaper. The article had a picture of a man holding either binoculars or a camera and told his story of how he became a private investigator. The article stated, "However, he will help someone whose estranged spouse has convinced the children to lie. He has worked on cases involving allegations that ranged from child abuse to a husband who supposedly liked to wear a black dress." Later in the article, it stated that his usual fee was $800 a day. Wow! Robert had money to pay someone to follow me, but couldn't pay child support. Go figure!

I would like to share the psychological test results and interpretations from the psychologist's report so that you can have an outside view about our family and form your own opinion. Please note that this is word for word and exactly as it was typed in the report on pages 17–21. I had to pay per page, so I couldn't afford the whole trial transcript.

Mrs. Parson

Mrs. Parson's test protocol suggests that she is an individual who functions effectively in most areas of her life. She answered items as most "normal" people do and is free of disabling psychopathology. Her test responses suggested a healthy balance between positive self-evaluation and self-criticism, indicating a psychologically well-adjusted individual with few overt signs of emotional disturbance. Mrs. Parson appears to have high intellectual ability with wide interests. She is capable of dealing with problems in her daily life in a versatile and often enterprising manner. She is clear-thinking, systematic, and approaches problems in a realistic manner. She is interested in people and presents as enthusiastic and verbally fluent.

Mrs. Parson is currently functioning under a high level of stress and her coping resources sometimes are in danger of being overwhelmed. At times, intense and transient anxiety impairs her perceptual accuracy, although there are no problems with her thought processes. She is able to handle complex material, although she may spend excessive energy processing environmental information. In decision-making, she prefers to delay a response until time has been taken to consider alternatives and their consequences, and to keep her emotions aside while doing so. She has a tendency to internalize her negative feelings which sometimes leaves her feeling tense and irritable. She is not always comfortable being around strong emotions, although she is well-controlled and modulated in her expression of her feelings, and is unlikely to act in an impulsive fashion.

Interpersonally, Mrs. Parson tends to be somewhat reserved when it comes to asking for assistance, and she is aware that people might think she is "too independent". Currently, she presents as somewhat cynical, anxious and self-protective regarding relationships, and has often felt unsupported and not properly helped by systems. She sometimes feels as though no-one listens to or cares for her and she suffers from "lack of love". At times, her self-esteem is low and she acknowledges feeling like a "failure" with respect to both marriage and a career. She is very protective toward her children and has a tendency to focus upon the needs of others rather than her own.

With respect to child-rearing, Mrs. Parson presented with no suggestions that she would behave in an abusive manner toward her children. She presented Olivia as the child with whom she has the most concern, portraying her as having difficulty adjusting to changes in her physical or social environment and as placing many demands on Mrs. Parson as a parent. Olivia is often irritable and unhappy and Mrs. Parson was open in stating that she sometimes feels that Olivia does not match what she expected in a girl. She is aware that she has a number of family difficulties and this is creating some degree of unhappiness in her current life.

Mr. Parson

Based on Mr. Parson's test protocol, it would not be unusual to discover that he has deviant social beliefs or practices. People who score as he did may manifest a severe neurotic or even psychotic condition. Mr. Parson harbors intense feelings of inferiority and insecurity and is generally an introverted and fearful individual. He lacks confidence and self-esteem, and presents as apathetic with a tendency toward withdrawal. It would not be unusual for Mr. Parson to express suicidal ideation. It is not easy for Mr. Parson to become emotionally involved with others as he is suspicious, distrustful, and avoids deep ties. He is seriously deficient in social skills and lives a lifestyle which might be described as schizoid. He suffers greatly when he engages in self-inspection, feeling that he falls short in comparison to others.

Terms such as moody, restless, dissatisfied and unstable might be used to describe Mr. Parson. He has a low frustration tolerance and explosive acting out tendencies due to inadequate constrictive controls which sometimes break down. At this time, strong feelings of anger and hostility are released. Although he has some organized coping resources, they are currently overwhelmed by unintegrated needs and drives. Emotions tend to be overly influential in Mr. Parson's life, and he may behave in a labile fashion. His thinking might be described as fragmented and illogical at times. It would not be unexpected for him to suffer from problems in attention, concentration, memory and judgment. He lacks effective coping strategies and may rely on primitive defenses such as denial and repression. At times, he may blur reality and fantasy and tends to become passive and withdrawn under stress. Mr. Parson tends to feel blamed and even persecuted by others, and sometimes engages in grandiose fantasies to boost his self-image.

In the area of child-rearing, Mr. Parson scored in a manner consistent with individuals who are known child abusers. He reported high levels of personal distress and a sense of having many problems coming from sources outside himself. He portrays his child Olivia as having difficulty adjusting to changes and being hard to relate to, as well as placing excessive demands on him as a parent. Mr. Parson also feels unsupported by others in his role as parent, and he is socially isolated such that neglect of child care responsibilities is a potential danger. He feels very angry and critical toward his ex-wife, and does not appear to have moved far in resolving his sense of loss vis-à-vis the marriage.

Conclusions & Recommendations

With respect to the issue of the sexual abuse of the children, it is unfortunately not possible to say in a definitive manner what has occurred. No incidents were directly witnessed, and medical evidence was not obtained. The fact that Olivia would not repeat the disclosures she had earlier made to Constable _____ is not unusual. Because the children have been interviewed on several occasions and because the interview process has been stressful for Olivia, it could be expected that she would be reluctant to discuss these issues again. Furthermore, Olivia is not too young to understand that the alleged activities of her father are inappropriate and that he could "get in trouble" for having engaged in them. As children typically remain attached and loyal to their caregivers, even in cases of abuse, that Olivia would be protective of her father by refusing to make a disclosure is also understandable. This attitude of protectiveness toward Mr. Parson was apparent in the comments of the boys as well. For example, before he was asked specifically about potential sexually inappropriate touching, Logan pointedly portrayed his father's behavior as innocent.

Nevertheless, the videotaped interview between Constable _____ and Olivia was strongly suggestive that Olivia has been sexually victimized by Mr. Parson. Furthermore, Olivia made a partial disclosure during the current assessment, indicating that her father had "peed on (her)". Her anxious and distressed emotional state during the interview was consistent with that of children who are confirmed victims of child sexual abuse. In addition, Mr. Parson's comments during the interview with the polygraph operator, although not direct confessions of wrongdoing, did not represent denials. He repeatedly spoke about his "problems" and displayed concern and anxiety about Mrs. Parson discovering his behavior with Olivia. His preoccupation with "what a child molester feels like" is also unusual and would not be expected from an individual who was not highly conflicted about this area and who may have already engaged in such activity. Because so many pressures have been put on the children regarding these kinds of disclosures, for example, being taped by police, private investigators, and Mr. Parson, it is unlikely that an undistorted disclosure of actual events could be obtained at this point.

A second issue addressed in the current assessment relates to each parent's capacity to function in the role of caretaker of the children. There is a general consensus that "good parenting" is related to a number of factors, and that decisions regarding placement of children should be made with consideration of the degree of congruence or "fit" between child needs and parental characteristics. In the area of emotional attachment, Mrs. Parson appears to be the more functional parent. Although she had a far from "perfect" childhood, she has developed enduring and lasting relationships with family members. Mr. Parson hails from a much more dysfunctional family and his early caretaking was disrupted with his move to foster care. He spoke repeatedly during the assessment about his inability to feel close to people and his frequent desires to abandon the children. On the variable of differentiation of self, Mr. Parson showed some deficiencies in his capacity to place the needs of the children first, and often focused on his own distress in the situation, rather than the effects on the children. This suggested some blurring of his interpersonal boundaries between self and others. Mrs. Parson appeared to have a better appreciation for a parent's need to protect the children by keeping her own issues well-contained.

With respect to accurate perceptions of child, Mr. Parson tended to use fairly global and superficial labels to describe the children. He indicated that his lack of awareness of many of their current needs and feelings is related to his estrangement from them; nevertheless, this exists and is significant. Mrs. Parson was able to draw clear distinctions between the children and capture their uniqueness and individuality of needs and issues in her descriptions of them. Another important factor is reasonable expectations of child. Mrs. Parson seemed to have a solid appreciation of the developmental needs and trends in her children, including past, current and future. She appreciated their needs to be protected from emotionally arousing material and for a consistent, safe and predictable environment. With respect to chores and responsibilities, Mr. Parson was not unreasonable. However, he did not seem to have a clear appreciation of the children's needs for firm and consistent limit-setting and protection of their emotions from undue stress, for example that related to the divorce and custody dispute.

Another important factor is the parents' communication skills. Mrs. Parson presents as verbally fluent and she was able to encourage the children to express their feelings in words. She showed a wide repertoire of interpersonal interactional skills and was able to support, contain, motivate and stimulate the children. Mr. Parson is much less at ease expressing himself verbally and often was non-responsive to the children. No doubt, some of this related to his hearing deficit, a very real factor underlying his communication difficulties. It is indeed unfortunate that Mr. Parson feels he is unable to tolerate the hearing aids which might render him more capable in the area of verbal communication. His repertoire of interpersonal skills was rather limited, and he tended to rely on physical and concrete methods of dealing with the children's behavior.

Parental availability is also an important factor, both at the present and what is anticipated for the future. Mr. Parson spoke repeatedly of his strong urge to "just walk away" and it has been alleged that he has exercised very sporadic access at times, despite the distress that this has caused the children, which they have communicated to him. It does not appear that these same concerns apply to Mrs. Parson, as she has remained physically and emotionally available to the children throughout their lives, and appears to appreciate their need for individualized attention. With regard to parental risk factors for abuse and neglect, psychological testing strongly suggests that Mr. Parson is at high risk for such behavior. His egocentrism, impulsivity, resentfulness of expectations and demands, and strong unintegrated aggressive feelings, coupled with ineffective, constrictive and rigid controls, place him at high risk for engaging in abusive behavior. Mrs. Parson's psychological test profile reveals no such concerns and, to the best of the examiner's knowledge, no concerns have been raised regarding her behavior vis-à-vis the children. Mrs. Parson has no overt signs of psychopathology but this cannot be said for Mr. Parson.

It is also important for a parent to support the child's needs for the other parent, something which was quite apparent in Mrs. Parson's comments, but less notable in those from Mr. Parson. He repeatedly referred to Mrs. Parson as "vicious" and talked about his desire to prove that she was a liar and to otherwise "beat her". Also important in assessing degree of fit are the parent's history as primary caretaker. In this case, it does not appear disputable that this has been Mrs. Parson's role. It is also important to consider child preferences especially for children over the age of 12. In the Parson matter, the children clearly expressed love, attachment and concern for each parent, and were very careful to avoid making any direct statements of preference. However, the occasional indirect comment, such as Kevin's belief that his father "really wouldn't care" if he lost their custody, and Nathan's statement that each child was "mom's kid," are suggestive that they feel more comfortable with their mother in the caretaking role.

In summary, it is clear that there is considerable animosity and dysfunction in the relationship between Mr. and Mrs. Parson, which mitigates against the possibility of a successful co-parenting arrangement. At the same time, research suggests that, in most cases, children benefit from continued contact with both parents. A notable exception would be those cases in which a parent was known to be abusing a child. Although this cannot be definitively stated to be the case in the Parson matter, there are enough suggestions that abuse might have occurred and suggestions that Mr. Parson has a personality profile that would render him at risk for further abuse, that this possibility cannot be dismissed. Furthermore, Mr. Parson's apparent pattern of inconsistent and conflicted access is also not healthy for the children.

At this point, it is recommended that custody remain in the hands of Mrs. Parson, with Mr. Parson to be offered specified and supervised access for a time-limited period during which his responses and the children's reaction to this arrangement can be evaluated. If he proves unwilling or unable to meet these obligations and to be a reliable and consistent figure in his children's lives, access might be reconsidered. If he does meet these conditions with no untoward effects on the children, altering the access to an unsupervised schedule might then be considered.

One month later was our trial. A week was set aside for our trial, but I believe it was over in three days. The female constable was called to the stand to state what Olivia had disclosed. I remember the judge asking her why no charges of sexual abuse were pressed against Robert. I don't remember her response. The polygraph operator was also called to the stand to state evidence that was disclosed during the test. Finally, the psychologist was called to the stand. She was the most credible witness I could ever ask for! (See, God did answer my prayers!) I was called to the stand and remember shaking, sweating, and at times feeling like I was going to pass out. There were a few times I broke down and the judge asked if I wanted time to compose myself.

Robert was called to the stand and questioned extensively. He was asked about what he said during the polygraph test and denied it. He was asked about statements he made to the psychologist and denied them also. It was brought up that he had told the psychologist he had twenty-seven witnesses lined up and access to $2.6 million to prove me a liar. The lawyer asked where the witnesses were now and why he didn't use the money to litigate. Robert said this fellow never came through with the money. Robert was questioned about his statement to the psychologist that if he went down for sexual abuse of the children, he would get out of prison he would go back in for two more crimes. Robert replied to this by saying he wasn't a violent man and never planned to hurt anyone. Then Robert explained that this was some of his self-help theory. Robert went on to say he treats himself, basically by getting his thoughts out so they are no longer a threat. The judge became upset with the line of questioning and told the lawyer that he hadn't made any notes since Robert was put on the stand.

The outcome was this: the judge said there was no evidence of any kind to change custody. Custody was affirmed to me with respect to all four children, as stated in the divorce nine months prior. However, the judge stated that the issue of access required "substantially more elaboration…The right to access was not really challenged but the real issue was to define the terms of access." He mentioned Robert's sporadic visitations, and the limited evidence before the court, but said he agreed with the psychologist's conclusion. He said that even though there was no positive evidence with regard to sexual abuse to the children, this did "not terminate the issues of child abuse." He said that "the fact that is has not been affirmatively established does not in this kind of case remove it as an element that can be considered by a Court." The judge also said, "The existence of smoke demands extreme care until the absence of real fire can be assured." The judge went on to say, "The greater evil would be the exposure of these children to what would be a room full of smoke."

The second item the judge discussed was Robert's failure to exercise the right of access. Again from the pages of the trial transcript, the judge said there was:

> ...no reasonable or acceptable explanation for that failure. That conduct, in itself, seems to belie general and genuine desire for access on his part. But—and this is perhaps the most important element—the children wanted to see him, and I am bound to add at this point that I have no doubt that these children love their father just as he has love for them. His failure to meet their desire for access to him has been distressing to the children. That's clear from the opinion of the psychologist. That distress, in my judgment, must be avoided for the benefit of the mental health of the children. If access is not going to be exercised by the father, it should be abolished. At least that would remove the children's expectation of it and the distress caused by failure of that expectation. In the result, there will be qualified access. The access will be on a limited and supervised basis. The limitation will be that the access will be for three consecutive hours on either a Saturday or a Sunday between the hours of 1:00 and 4:00 p.m. That will occur twice monthly only. The days will be selected by the father on reasonable notice both to the mother and to the supervisor. The supervisor of access shall be a disinterested person selected by the Director of Child Welfare. The expense of supervision shall be borne by the Director of Child Welfare. For a period of six months, there should be no application by any party to vary this order unless leave of the Court is first obtained to issue an appropriate Notice of Motion seeking that variation.
>
> It is, clearly, going to be up to the father as to whether his right is, in due course, extended or further curtailed, if indeed not abolished. That is bound to depend at least in part on how the father exercises his right of access and what professional guidance he obtains to clear the smoke.

Thank you, thank you, God! I finally got a court order giving Robert supervised access only. The children would finally be protected. That's all I wanted. I just wanted to protect my children.

You'll never guess what happened next. Social Services appealed. Can you believe it? I finally get someone to listen and give supervised access, and now I have to go back to court again by the same people who originally helped me get the change. Unbelievable! Actually, it turned out the only thing they really wanted changed was the part that Child Welfare was responsible for paying for the access. They did not want to be locked into this indefinitely. However, the judge dismissed this appeal.

CHAPTER ELEVEN

ROBERT TOOK ME BACK TO COURT A FEW MONTHS LATER TO LOWER the child support payments to $25 per child, per month. Robert had quit his job because his employer was garnishing his wages and told him he wouldn't be paid for the job he had just completed. Once again, Robert got the arrears cancelled but the payments were not lowered. They would remain at $150 per child, per month. This was getting ridiculous. Even though there were orders to pay, Robert wasn't paying and was going back every six to twelve months and would get the arrears cancelled. Insane! What was the point in having a court order?

Six months later, I found myself back in court again. Robert wanted unsupervised access. He had actually been seeing the children regularly every two weeks under supervision. However, he was not seeking any professional help at all. Child Welfare presented an affidavit and stated they were opposed to no supervision. The judge dismissed Robert's application and added that Robert would not be able to bring any further application to vary the terms of access unless and until a counselor or psychologist treating Robert indicated in a written opinion that unsupervised access was recommended.

Meanwhile, Kevin was really struggling in school. He'd had four detentions and the principal called and said he was at a high risk of being expelled. Robert was continually making and breaking promises to the children, like promising to buy Kevin a motorcycle, or taking them to West Edmonton Mall or buying certain presents. Robert had told the kids he would keep going to court and to get full custody of them.

Robert also told the children he intended to kill me. I took the children to the police station to file a report of this threat. Unfortunately, I was told there wasn't much they could do because the threat wasn't told directly to me. They said they could talk to Robert, but there was a good chance it would only escalate his anger towards me.

I took Kevin to a counselor again, and Kevin said he didn't want to be alone with Dad. Kevin talked about suicide a lot and one evening when we were driving somewhere he opened the car door and attempted to jump out, but Logan hung onto him and screamed. There was no way I could help him or any of the children. I had attempted counseling numerous times with the children and none of them would open up about anything, and they cried and created a fuss about going. I was told to back off, that they would talk when they were good and ready and there was a good chance it may never happen or would perhaps happen later in adulthood.

When Kevin was around thirteen, he exploded at home, slamming kitchen cupboards and hollering. I tried to calm him down.

He kept shouting at me, "You don't know, Mom. You have no idea what I went through. You can't tell me to stop being angry when you don't even know how much anger I have. You don't even know what really happened to me. You weren't there and you didn't even help me. You don't know how many times I heard Olivia crying and screaming and that I'd walk in and see Dad on top of her and try to pull him off and then Dad would throw me out and kick me and lock the door and I'd have to listen to Olivia scream more and couldn't help her, couldn't rescue her!"

I was stunned and felt like my breath was taken away. Like someone kicked me in my gut. I had no idea how much pressure was on Kevin, how much he had seen and heard and how helpless he felt.

I felt so useless. I was an awful parent. I could love and love them to death, but I could not take their pain away. I couldn't fix this. I couldn't make them happy. I couldn't make them feel better. What kind of a mom was I?

I carried on trying to be the best Mom I could. All four children were in soccer by the time they were four years old. I worked full-time, would rush home to get them supper and drive to their respective soccer fields. If two children played the same night, I would watch half of one game, and then grab the two children who weren't playing and drive to the other soccer field and watch the last half of the other child's game and then collect the three and drive back to pick up the first child. The coaches used to tell me the children played so much better while I was watching, but to be fair I tried to split myself in half. Then we'd go home to work on homework, bathe, and get to bed. When all four played soccer we went four nights a week.

In the summer holidays, I would come home and pack a picnic and take the children to a park and let them play a few hours, then head home for baths and bed. Holidays? Well, I really had no money to speak of, but I tried to make the best of my imagination. I would save for a one-night stay in a hotel at a provincial park and would take an electric frying pan. I would cook soup for lunch, hamburgers for supper, popcorn for snacks—thank goodness for the versatility of a simple frying pan! We'd go to the beach for the afternoon, go for hikes, play mini-golf, etc. There were a few times someone lent me a tent, and that helped cut costs.

I sent all four children to Bible Camp, the same one where I grew up. It was about five hundred kilometers away. Getting them to camp became quite a challenge and cost. When the children were older, some would go the first week and I'd take them, come back, and the following weekend pick them up and drop off the others, come back, and then the next weekend go again to pick up the older ones. This meant an expense of travelling three weekends in a row. It was so worth it, though. In fact, all four attended up until their grade 12 graduation. Other than that, I couldn't afford anything extravagant. The children were happy though with just spending time with me and away from the house. I bought the children a trampoline—one of the first ones in our neighborhood. At that time it was about $1,800—now they are only a few hundred. I used my child tax credit for clothes, books, sports, and savings for camp and the trampoline, as well as a few trips to the city where we stayed with a friend. While we were in the city, I took the children to the Zoo, Calaway amusement park, the wave pool, and Heritage Park—all which were major events for a single mom with four little ones, but I wanted to give my children as many opportunities as possible in spite of my low income.

I approached our church about a Big Brothers/Sisters program. I explained that I didn't trust many people and the waiting period was phenomenal at our community Big Brothers/Sisters program. My children desperately needed a male companion. The church declined my suggestion and wouldn't even consider looking into it or even asking if someone in the church might be interested. I asked if I could start a singles Bible study. I wasn't given much enthusiastic response, so I took it on as a challenge and started putting up bulletins and asking for singles' names within the church.

I told the few contacts I had that there would be an open house at my place on a certain date. Much to my surprise, more than ten people came, looking for friends and a Bible study where others could relate to them. I went back to the church and asked if we could use a room at the church once a week. This was approved and a coffee machine was set up for us. I arranged for a babysitter once a week and got the Bible study underway.

There were times when we had more than twenty attend from all over the city, not just from our church. I soon learned that people weren't ready to go home after the study, so I approached a restaurant and asked if we could reserve a long table one evening a week for coffee. Of course we went through growing pains; some people looking for a mate, some just checking us out to see how "religious" our group was, some condemning the form of Bible study we were having, getting sidetracked on major discussions of people's opinion or interpretation of the Bible and so on. I would arrange for potlucks with our children, evenings at the park, ball games, New Year's Eve parties at the hotel with a waterslide, and setting up an ongoing plan for cheap movie night: we would stand outside the theater and whoever showed up from the group would have someone to sit with.

In spite of who Robert was, he had no problem attracting women. He had girlfriend after girlfriend. He had been with a lady who had one little girl. Then this lady got pregnant and my children now have a half-brother. Get this: this young lady came to see me in my office. She said she had always disliked me because of what Robert had told her about me and our marriage. However, now she was beginning to wonder if I had been telling the truth. She asked for my help. She wanted me to go to court with her, because she thought her daughter had been sexually assaulted by Robert. I asked her why she thought that. She told me that her daughter, who was only a few years old, was sitting on the floor in her shorts and her Grandma was there with her. Her daughter had a box of Smarties and they watched her put Smarties up her vagina. The grandma asked what on earth she was doing. The little girl explained that it was okay, that some were for her and the rest for Daddy! I don't know if she ever took him to court. We were invited to the son's birthday party for a couple years, but have not seen them in several years.

Three years after our trial, Child Welfare went back to court so that they wouldn't have to pay for the supervision any longer. This was granted. Robert would have to pay for his own supervisor. He saw the children less and less. Robert finally told the children he was moving out of the city and that if he didn't move, someone would die. The children were about thirteen, eleven, nine and seven at the time. We had no phone number or way of contacting Robert and didn't hear from him for years after that.

CHAPTER TWELVE

KEVIN WAS EIGHTEEN AND WORKING AT A LOCAL RESTAURANT IN the kitchen. One of the waitresses went back into the kitchen and told Kevin there was a man asking for him.

Kevin peeked through the kitchen door and told the waitress he didn't know him and couldn't be bothered. The waitress went back to the man and explained this. The man told her to go back and tell him he was his dad.

Kevin told the waitress he wasn't interested in seeing him and asked him to leave. Kevin called me at home, extremely upset, and told me he was phoning to say goodbye. I asked him what was going on and he told me Robert had been there and he was going to find him and kill him and knew he'd be going to prison. He said he wanted it over—just over.

I tried to tell him it wasn't worth it. I cried and begged him to listen. I told him Robert had already taken so many years of our lives and why would he allow him to take the rest of his life by sending him to prison for murder.

I immediately called the restaurant and asked to talk to the manager. The manager was well aware of how upset Kevin was and how he was pacing and beside himself. I wanted to call the police. I felt it would be better to save Kevin from doing something stupid than to lose him forever! I knelt down and prayed and begged God to give me the words to say. I got up and called Kevin back. I suggested that maybe Robert was coming back to apologize, or maybe he was sick and dying, or maybe he had money he wanted to share with him or maybe…who knows what.

I told Kevin I could phone some old friends from my past and perhaps find Robert—that they could meet in a public place and have coffee and then see what his feelings were towards him and why he was here.

Much to my surprise, Kevin agreed. I contacted some old friends and they knew where Robert was. I suggested a time and Kevin's restaurant to meet the following day. I called Kevin back and he seemed much more settled. I told him to tell his manager and make sure someone kept an eye on them so the meeting wouldn't get out of hand.

The following day was actually Father's Day—how ironic! They met and Kevin said he was shaking and so nervous, and that Robert was nervous too. He said Robert made a bunch of promises to him again—a motorcycle (again!), money, etc. Kevin said he felt relief like he had never felt before. Kevin said Robert wasn't worth it—not even worth killing him—and was so glad I stepped in and found a solution. Kevin changed a lot after this. A lot of his anger subsided and he seemed happier and more in control.

When Olivia was around twenty, she started phoning me about her nightmares. She started out by telling me about how she felt like she was in prison and she couldn't go back to sleep. The dreams were escalating and she was losing more and more sleep and having panic attacks and stomach problems. I asked her to start writing down what she remembered from the dreams. She described to me how she would be hanging on to bars, as if in prison, screaming and screaming to get out, but couldn't.

I asked her to describe her surroundings. She said the walls were yellow and there was something around the top, close to the ceiling. She described a stand she thought she could reach by a window. She said she felt that if she could just reach the stand, and step on it, then she could escape through the window. She also said there were two open doors but they didn't lead anywhere.

I listened intently and my heart was racing. She was describing her baby room to a T. Her bedroom had been yellow with a baby border around the top. The change table was under the window. The closet doors were open because the spring was broken. The bars would have been her crib. I explained her nightmare to her. I shared that I had been told years earlier that she would probably start remembering things if there was a trigger—smells, male relationships, certain comments, whatever would trigger things from her past.

Olivia is not sure how to handle this all. She doesn't want to remember—just doesn't want to remember it at all. She's scared to face what really happened to her. Sometimes she asks if she can press charges all these years later and then wonders if it would even be worth it. We don't even know how to contact Robert or where he is.

Well, the unexpected happened again. Money appeared in my bank account and the abbreviation on the bank statement said MEP. I had no idea what this was until I sat and really thought about it, and it suddenly dawned on me what the abbreviation stood for. It was Maintenance Enforcement Program—a government agency who collects child support payments if you've registered your account through them. I still had the same bank account, believe it or not. It had been fourteen years since I had received anything through his wages being garnisheed. Now I was suddenly receiving around $350 a month. This could only mean he was working again and I knew he had a national garnishee on him. The children were grown and here I was, collecting again.

That was not the most unexpected thing. After I had been receiving money sporadically for about two years, I received a phone call at work from Maintenance Enforcement. The lady said she was updating her file and wanted to make sure everything was accurate for court next week. I stopped her and said, "Pardon me. What court? What are you talking about?"

She was taken back and couldn't believe I hadn't been served yet. She read part of the notice they received and advised me that Robert was taking me back to court, within a few days, fifteen years later, to cancel all the child support arrears. She told me to go to court and see if I could get a copy of his application. I knew from past experience that I would have to ask for a postponement because I wouldn't have time to respond and serve him prior the court date.

Here we go again. How dare he stir up old memories and put the fear back in me! I began to close all the blinds at home, lock the door, and set the alarm constantly and hide in my bedroom. The nightmares were back, and all I kept remembering was his last comment to the children about killing me if he didn't leave town and how he told others about cutting me up into pieces and hanging me in the basement.

I read his affidavit. His reasons for the application were: he doesn't want to be a burden on society, wants his financial future assured, the children are now adults, that he doesn't have enough money, that he owed child support for his other son, that he should be reimbursed for years of not seeing the children and that access was restricted due to something he did not do and was never proven. He submitted three years of T4s showing his incomes of $55,000, $74,000, and $63,000. He shared his monthly budget showing a vehicle loan payment for $880 (total loan $12,000), credit card payment of $100 (total owing $600), financial institution for $400 (total owing $4,000), and get this: $375 for alcohol/tobacco. The balance of his budget left a credit of $405.

I contacted my four children. I didn't want to put them through pain again, but felt they were all adults and had a right to know what was going on. It was now 2008 and they were 28, 26, 24, and 22. I never dreamt any of them would come home, but Kevin and Olivia came for the court hearing. Kevin came for moral support for me and said he didn't even want to talk to Robert. Olivia, however, had a million mixed emotions.

The judge dismissed the claim. Yeah! However, as we left the court room, Olivia turned around and went back in and came out with Robert. She proceeded to attack him verbally. She never even mentioned the sexual abuse, just that he was an absentee father and how dare he be so mean to them and she pointed out how she adored Kevin and how he doesn't even know his own children. She was hollering so loud and shaking and finally broke down and the tears were rolling. I thought we were going to be removed from the court house.

Kevin finally went over and wrapped his loving arms around her and literally picked her up and dragged her out. I proceeded to walk out and Robert stepped up beside me. He told me what a beautiful girl Olivia had become. Really, this is all he got from everything she said to him?

I said, "Yes," and picked up my pace to get out as fast as I could.

As we were about to go different directions, Robert said he wished me well and that he harbored no hard feelings against me. I was shaking and couldn't get away from him fast enough! I caught up to Kevin and Olivia and we all hugged each other and said we were glad it was over. They had a long drive back and didn't even stay for coffee to discuss anything that happened—just that they were glad I won.

Olivia phoned home a lot and said she was glad she came to confront him. She said she felt great—absolutely great. However, a few weeks later, her nightmares began again and she was getting more and more upset.

It's so hard. I still can't help. How useless I feel, all over again! I ache and hurt so much for her. How I wish I could make things better and take all the pain away.

CHAPTER THIRTEEN

ALMOST A YEAR TO THE DATE, I RECEIVED ANOTHER CALL FROM Maintenance Enforcement. I was going back to court again. Once again, Robert never served me and he didn't take the proper procedures to have Maintenance Enforcement serve me, so they called to tell me the court date was a few days away and I'd better go to court or he could win. I was out of town and my time away was cut short in order to deal with this again. When will it ever end!

So, we went back to court. The lawyer for Maintenance Enforcement stated that he thought this application should not even be looked at because it had been denied last year and nothing had changed. The judge talked to Robert and said the arrears would "not go away" but if he was having trouble making payments, he should make arrangements with MEP and not the Court of Queen's Bench. Robert was vividly upset and grabbed his paperwork and stormed out of the court room.

This time Robert's reason for asking for the arrears cancellation was mainly his drastic drop of income. However, he had a lengthy affidavit with fifty-seven points, such as: causing hardship due to lower income, another court order for support for another son, talking about denied access from 15 years ago, denying the sexual accusations from the past, denying his threats of wanting to kill me, stating he's not a violent person and has never been convicted of anything, denying he was behind on support payments in the past, stating that he left me matrimonial property (sold long before we ever separated), that he never stayed hidden as I had stated last year (and yet Maintenance Enforcement had no address for 15 years), that he was about to be evicted due to late rental payments, that the city he lives in has a high cost of living and that the court refuses to listen to him.

Of course, pretty soon Robert was back to sending no payments. It was good for the short time it lasted!

PART II

CHAPTER FOURTEEN

NOW I'M GOING TO TAKE US BACK A WHILE, TO PICK UP AFTER THE end of my relationship with Robert. Life went on with me being a very busy single mom. We moved into a rental home and the children changed schools. Several neighbors commented about how well behaved the children were and how impressed they were that we all pulled together. I would be seen outside showing the boys how to start and push the lawnmower. We had a huge yard. I would only get them to do a little, because they were still very young, but I wanted them to learn how to work and wanted them to know we were a team and needed each other.

Lots of their friends called me Mom. Our yard was extremely popular because of the trampoline and the other children seemed to know when I was baking homemade buns, doughnuts, or whatever. Some days, when I was baking, I thought my children put a sign outside because the house and yard were full with hungry visitors.

My children made their beds the day they started kindergarten, kept their rooms fairly clean, helped with dusting and helped with dishes.

The visits or lack of visits by their father and court cases were a never-ending problem.

I've looked back at my income and wonder how I ever survived raising four little ones. I know it was by the grace of God that we could keep going. In fact, the children have asked the same question on different occasions recently. I know they're struggling now on their incomes, and trying to imagine how we survived. It was hard for them to miss out on so many things, but the one thing that remained constant was my love for them and they knew that.

I had the wonderful opportunity to pray with each child nightly. I remember getting down on our knees and them praying for their daddy. Oh, how I struggled with that. I didn't think Robert deserved their prayers, their forgiveness, or God's forgiveness.

It took me a long time to truly forgive him, until one day, while I was alone and on my knees, I felt God telling me that the best thing that could ever happen to our family would be for Robert to truly give his life to the Lord, admit his wrongs to us, and ask us for forgiveness. That could truly bring healing to our whole family. I began to pray for him like never before!

I was also blessed with each child asking me for help to pray to ask Jesus into their hearts. What a privilege of a lifetime! Don't get me wrong, I haven't forgotten what Robert did to us, but I truly had to forgive in order to move on.

I started going out about three years after the separation. There wasn't much to do in our city. A girlfriend asked me to go dancing. Well, I had never danced before and had no clue how. She laughed and said she'd teach me. Of course the only place to dance was the bar. I had never been part of that scene. I wasn't a drinker. In fact, I didn't even know the names of drinks and didn't have a clue what would taste good and what I should order. I tried one and would occasionally order the same one. I really didn't like alcohol, so why bother. I didn't need a drink to be happy, so a lot of times I only had coke.

I became the designated driver for the two of us. She laughed at how I danced and said she needed to work with me. I had no rhythm. That was strange, because I play the piano and sing. My girlfriend was pretty and was showered with attention. We used to have lots of men come sit with us and ask her to dance. A few would ask me to dance, but soon found out I was no good at it. I did learn a bit of country dancing though, and some guys would take pity on me sitting alone and ask me to dance at least once each time we went out.

We wouldn't go out until the children were sleeping. That way I was still able to bathe them and tuck them in. It didn't matter how late we got home, I still was up early and got the children ready for Sunday school and church the following morning.

I vowed I would never get into another relationship. I didn't trust anyone and was quite content on my own. I was extremely independent—changed the car tires by myself, mowed the lawn, started the pilot light on the furnace if it went out, shoveled snow, and took care of whatever else needed to be done. I remember a couple of single, male neighbors would wander over on numerous occasions to offer assistance, but I was too stubborn to accept it.

I did go to counseling to cope with the divorce and figure out how I could help my children. I remember one of the counselors asking me about my family history. I said I had two brothers and two sisters. However, on numerous occasions I guess I would say something in regards to having five siblings. Finally he asked me if I had ever lost a sibling in some way. I shared how my oldest brother, seventeen years older than me, had been married and had a son and his wife died a couple days after child birth due to complications. I explained that my parents raised his son until he was seven years old.

I began grieving. Oh, the grief was overwhelming, sometimes almost unbearable! As I opened up to the counselor, I realized I had never grieved the loss of my honourary sibling before. You see, my parents raised him until my brother remarried seven years later and took him back. We were told not to cry and just to say goodbye so it wouldn't be so difficult for him when they left.

I never saw my parents shed a tear; not a one! I remember, as a child, crying myself to sleep and wondering why or how they could just give him away. I would have been thirteen at the time. He was my little brother, as far as I was concerned. I remember wondering if my parents would give me away too. What if I was bad? What if they got mad at me?

I think it was around this time and the following few years that I struggled more in school and had more health issues. I remember desperately looking for attention from outsiders, to the point of lying and telling others I had cancer just to see if anyone would care in case my parents gave me away. I wondered where I would go and who would take care of me. Eventually my stories got back to my parents and they were very angry and asked why I was lying and what they ever did to me to deserve this! They didn't get it. They just didn't get it. They had no idea what their decision to give back my brother/nephew did to me.

Actually, I also had no idea why I was telling the stories. I had no idea I was grieving or why I was feeling so unwanted and lost. The counselor suggested I go and talk to my parents about this, more than seventeen years later. However, I did drive home one weekend and after my children were sleeping, I told Mom and Dad I needed to talk to them. I brought up my concerns and we discussed it for hours. I found out my Mom would get up, drive the school bus, come home and go to her bedroom and cry for the whole day until Dad would come in and force her to take the bus to town to pick up the school children. I found out they had struggled so much, but kept it secret to protect us. Little did they know that we needed to see them hurt so we could have permission to cry and hurt also. What we don't do to protect our children, and how wrong it is sometimes!

Why am I telling you this? Well, when this came out in my counseling, I began wondering if that's why my parents wouldn't really listen to me about Robert. Perhaps they thought I was making it up. I know it was extremely difficult to imagine that a dad could sexually touch his own children. However, after I sent them proof of conversations in court and the psychologist report, they were shocked and extremely supportive to me.

CHAPTER FIFTEEN

I GOT INVOLVED WITH VICTIMS ASSISTANCE AT OUR LOCAL POLICE station. I made arrangements with a couple friends and neighbors to babysit the children. I went through a couple months of training and then was a volunteer one evening a week. I kept thinking I didn't go through this divorce for nothing; perhaps I could help someone else. I took training in domestic abuse, suicide, grief, divorce, blended families, teenage runaways, accidents, support to next of kin after notification of a death, and numerous situations the police would be notified of. This volunteer work gave me fulfillment; I could reach out and help someone else, in spite of my helplessness in reaching my own children.

I told you before that I started a singles Bible study at our church. On one of the movie nights, there was a movie I really wanted to see but would never go to alone. So I decided to get a sitter and stood outside the theater and waited to see if anyone from the Bible study group would show up. There was one guy, Donald, who showed up; however, there was no way I wanted to go to a movie alone with him. That would be too much like a date and there was no way I was going to do that. We stood and talked outside for quite a while and he finally convinced me that we should go see the movie.

When the movie was over, he asked me out for coffee. He already knew quite a bit about me from attending the same Bible study, but we both opened up a little more about our personal lives. He asked if we could hang out outside of the group. I told him I hadn't gotten involved with the group in order to date, and I didn't think it would be wise. We already had a few people in the group who dated, split up, and never came back. I didn't want that for me. After all, I was the one who started the group, saw a need for it, and didn't want to hinder that in any way.

I was shocked to find out that Donald had been a counselor at the same camp my children attended and later discovered that people from my home town knew him. I realized how much knowledge Donald had in biblical studies. He had attended a Bible school (same one I attended) for 3.5 years and was working towards his Bachelor's Degree in Religion. He had full intentions of becoming a pastor, however, the denomination he wanted to pastor in did not accept divorced people. Donald had been divorced for several years, had two boys with his ex that he rarely got to see, had closed his electrical business and was starting it over here. He was more than willing to help and lead the Bible study. That helped me a lot. At least I didn't have to do all the preparation and studying at home; I could just attend each week and plan the social events.

Soon Donald started coming over to my home. He would stop in to visit, watch TV, get to know the children, go for walks with the children and me, would take us all canoeing, and would try to bring us a meal—which I usually returned to him or conveniently left the house if I knew he was trying to drop one off, because I wasn't going to take handouts from anyone.

It didn't take long for our relationship to grow. We phoned each other a lot, shared our struggles with our first marriages, discussed the children, our jobs, our immediate families and became quite comfortable with each other. The children were hesitant in sharing a close relationship with any man. Olivia would not sit near him and would watch him from a distance and was very clingy to me. The boys, however, enjoyed the roughhousing and having a male figure around on occasion.

It was six months later. I had taken the children on a camping trip and much to my surprise, Donald drove out to find us. He spent an afternoon with us and then I thought he left. However, the next morning he showed up at our campsite again. Turns out he slept in his car and wanted to be with us the following day. That was the first time we held hands—six months after our first movie together. No one in the Bible study knew we were seeing each other.

Things progressed rather quickly after this. However, I was having major issues with fear and questioning whether I truly wanted a relationship. I had read numerous articles on second marriages and books about blended families. The success ratio was not great—not great at all. In fact, if you married an abuser, the chance of marrying another abuser was about 85%! I had a police check done, questioned church people who knew Donald for years, spoke to the pastor who had married Donald the first time, and spoke to family members and people from his Bible college. No one alerted me to any issues at all—no one! I was watching him so closely with the children to see if there were any signs of sexual abuse. I absolutely would *not* leave him alone with any of them.

I was also struggling with whether I could remarry—from my religious viewpoint. I finally had one pastor tell me Robert had committed adultery by having sex with the children and that he had lived with a few women since we separated, and thus I was free to remarry.

Donald had taken me alone and then with the children, to see his parents and family. They had a cottage and we went there also. The children loved being in the water and having the freedom to run around. His parents were very pleasant to all of us. His siblings and spouses were wonderful and I was quickly becoming attached to them.

Donald had told me how hard his dad was on him. He said they didn't have the best relationship. He recalled how driven his dad was and how much he pushed him to do more as a child. He described how his divorce affected everyone, how his religious beliefs differed and angered his dad, how his failure with his business upset his dad, and how he could never be good enough for him.

About three months later, I had taken a day off work and was home studying for an exam. Donald came over and we talked for quite a while. Suddenly, he got off the couch and down on his knee and said, "So, what if I asked you to marry me? What would you say?"

I laughed and said I would probably say yes.

He pulled out a washer—yes, a washer (you know, as in a nut, bolt, and washer) and placed it on my finger. I laughed so hard and told him I'd never take it off and then told him to leave so I could get busy and get some studying done. He looked at me, still on his knee, and proceeded to take the washer off my finger and while still holding my hand, replaced the washer with a real ring. We were engaged!

This was when we finally shared our relationship with everyone in the singles group and they were shocked at how private we had kept it and wondered how long it had been going on. They had no idea we had been dating for ten months.

I honestly thought we had covered every possible subject. I didn't want any stones left unturned. I was going into this with my eyes wide open and I didn't want to be caught off guard in any way. I asked him about child support to his two boys and he told me how much he had to pay each month. He didn't have to pay alimony to his ex-wife. I asked him about his business. I knew he was starting over and didn't have any money, but that didn't concern me. I wasn't after wealth. I just wanted someone to love the Lord, me, and my children. I was impressed that he had been to Mexico to work in an orphanage for a while. I was absolutely thrilled that he enjoyed singing and we had already sat at the piano and sang together a lot and enjoyed harmonizing. I've always taken out my frustrations as well as my happy moods on the piano. I won't sing a song unless I've studied the words and they truly apply to me.

I loved the fact that he was still considering the ministry in some form or another. My mother always said that she thought I'd marry a preacher. Donald seemed to enjoy being with the children and they were getting more and more used to having him around and were shining up to him.

He told me he wanted to get married on February 29—that was only 3.5 months away. We discussed it and it seemed too rushed for me. He said there was no reason to wait and we wouldn't have a big wedding anyway. I assumed we would get married in the church the children and I were attending. He said absolutely not! I questioned him and he made it perfectly clear that we would marry and attend the church he had been going to for several years.

It was the same denomination so it was no big deal; however, there were five of us and only one of him. Why should I be forced to take my children away from their familiar Sunday school, from their children's choir they were all involved in, from other relatives? Hadn't my children been ripped apart enough and moved and moved over again? Tell me, why should we all have to change just for him? Who did he think he was? He looked at me and said it wasn't open for discussion.

I couldn't believe what I was hearing. I looked at him and said, "You've got to be kidding. Are you telling me the engagement is off if we don't attend *your* church?"

He nodded and said it was his church or nothing.

I know what you're thinking. That should have been my first clue, right? Well, stupid me. I was offended and extremely hurt. However, I had gone to his church with him for several months and everyone was friendly and accepting of me and the children. Maybe it wouldn't be so bad. The big issue here was that I had vowed, to myself, years ago that I would never attend a really small church because I wanted my children to have other Christian friends to hang out with. I grew up in a community where I was the only one my age in our church and I struggled a lot keeping my faith and feeling very alone. I vowed I'd never do that to my children, especially living in a bigger city and having more opportunities. I wanted them to have more than I did. I wanted them to have places to go and things to do when I said no in their teen years to things I disagreed with. Did I listen to my conscience? Of course not. This was one small little thing. I could compromise on this, couldn't I?

We went to Donald's parents to tell them of our engagement. I remember it so vividly. We were finishing a meal and his dad asked Donald and me to come downstairs with him. He said the children could remain at the table. I remember getting looks of despair from others at the table. Once we got downstairs, his dad proceeded to tell Donald that he didn't think the marriage was a good idea. He asked me why my first marriage ended. I told him and he looked at Donald and said, "She'll do the same thing to you. She'll accuse you of something also. Don't do this." Donald looked at him and said that he didn't need his blessings, that we came home just to share the news.

I had taken Donald home to meet my parents several times and to introduce him to my siblings also. He was well accepted and I think my dad was actually relieved that I found a Christian man to love and someone to help me take care of the children. I remember asking several of them for their honest opinion. I asked if they could see something wrong with the relationship, perhaps something I was overlooking. No one said anything, not a word.

Chapter Sixteen

DONALD AND I HAD DISCUSSED OUR PRIOR MARRIAGES AND WHAT went wrong. He told me how his prior wife had cheated on him. He told me how she was running around with men and how difficult she was making it for him to see their two boys. He said he was lucky if he could talk to them on the phone and knew that they wouldn't be at the wedding even though we sent an announcement to them. He said he had a part in the marital problems, but she had refused to forgive and take him back. He said she was remarried and thus he was biblically free to remarry and move on. He went on to explain that he had made a new commitment to the Lord and believed our marriage was part of God's plan.

(He had all the right words for me.)

We set the date for February 29. We sent out homemade announcements, not invitations. We just wanted friends and family to know we were getting married. I sewed my dress, my bridesmaid's dress, Olivia's dress, the boys' shirts and ties, and Donald's shirt and tie. I made the floral arrangement for myself. Then we asked a restaurant if we could reserve a section and had put on our announcement that anyone could join us at their own expense. The restaurant owner said he'd make a wonderful smorg for us. This was the same restaurant where we met every week with the singles Bible study group for coffee.

My four children walked me down the aisle. Donald and I practiced and sang a couple duets during the ceremony. The pastor who married us was the same one that had done the ceremony for Donald's first wedding. He encouraged the marriage and gave me no warning signs I should be aware of.

We were both renting and both our places were too small. We began looking for a home to buy prior to getting married—in the same area as I was, so the children wouldn't have to change schools and friends again. We bought a modest, tiny two-bedroom home and added three small bedrooms in the basement. It was cute and I loved it. The children and I moved in right away and got settled.

A week before the wedding, we moved most of Donald's things over. When I was in the kitchen rummaging through his boxes, I became extremely frustrated. I was having a hard time overlooking how old and junky some of his dishes and kitchen things were. I didn't want to offend him, but I really didn't want his stuff in my cupboards. I had more than enough dishes without adding his to my collection.

I remember him walking in and seeing my tears and asking what was wrong. I explained to him that I didn't know where to put everything and he took one sweep with his arm and swiped the dishes all on the floor into a million pieces. He looked at me and said, "There, now you don't have to worry about it," and walked out.

I stood there shaking in total shock. What on earth was his problem? There was glass everywhere. I bent down to start scooping up the mess and began sobbing. Was I just emotional because of the move and the upcoming wedding, or was there more to this? Was this his way of solving problems? Wipe it away and not discuss it? Why was I struggling with adding his things to my collection? I know I am a neat freak and I thought I pretty much had the house in order before my parents and family would come, but why was I suddenly seeing a different side to Donald?

I was second-guessing our decision to marry. After the children went to bed, Donald stayed and visited for a while. I discussed my concerns and fears and he brushed it off again as just being wedding jitters. He said things would calm down once we were married and living under the same roof.

I prayed and prayed so much that night, begging God to give me a definitive answer whether Donald was the right man for me and the children or I was making another mistake. I begged Him to show me before it was too late, or was He already showing me and I was refusing to listen?

February 29 came and we were wed. An astonishing amount of people came to wish us well; just about everyone from the singles group, many from Victims Assistance, friends, extended family and immediate family. Donald's parents did not come. They had made it perfectly clear that they had other plans when we told them the date. That hurt me, but Donald said they were making a statement: that they didn't approve and wouldn't promote something they didn't believe in. Donald's sister and three brothers came and their spouses and families.

The children were excited to have a man in the house. They would have been twelve, ten, eight, and almost six. Logan idolized Donald. He admired his knowledge of the Bible and commended him for taking on four children who weren't his. Olivia was adjusting to having Donald in the house and on occasion would even sit beside him and allow him to cuddle her. Kevin and Nathan were okay with the relationship and didn't show any prior signs of rejection or fear of the marriage.

Three months.

Only three months later, my worst nightmare was unfolding. Donald told me the children had disobeyed him and needed to be punished. We had discussed discipline prior to getting married. We decided that ultimately it was my decision, however we both agreed that if I wasn't there when something happened, that he would have to take action and stop whatever the problem was.

I remember being in the kitchen and him telling me he needed to address something the children had done wrong while I had been out. He took all four children into our bedroom and locked the door. Soon I heard screaming, intense screaming. He was spanking the children, one at a time, in front of each other.

I couldn't get in. I banged and banged on the door and couldn't get in. I could hear the spanking, the screaming of the one being spanked and the screams of the other children watching and demanding him to stop.

It was over in minutes. Donald walked out and came into the kitchen and sat down at the table where I was sitting and crying. He laid his hands on the table, chuckled a little, and turned his palms upwards displaying blood running from them. I looked at him in absolute horror and asked what on earth he had done. I ran into the bedroom to comfort the children and they ran from me. I followed them to their rooms and explained that I tried getting in but the door was locked and they still wouldn't talk to me.

I stumbled back upstairs and told Donald I was calling the police. I proceeded into our bedroom, locked the door behind me, and dialed 911. When the operator answered I panicked and said I had the wrong number and hung up. I got down on my knees by our bed and sobbed and cried out to God.

"Why God? Why? I begged you to show me anything I should be aware of *before* marriage. Why God? Why?" I sobbed uncontrollably and reached once again for the phone. Do I report him? Are his bleeding hands going to prove anything? Will he go to jail or return to us and bring us more harm? The police never believed me in the first marriage. What if they don't lock him up? What if I have to face him and he comes right home?

Suddenly Donald was in the bedroom. How? He used a nail to push through the door knob and unlocked it. He came in and sat beside me and asked if I was okay. I looked at him in total shock and disgust. Of course I wasn't okay. Who are you kidding? He told me it wasn't as bad as it looked and the children will now understand that they need to obey him and that he means business when he asks them to do something.

I told him I chose the wrong man, that I was *very* wrong about him, that I didn't want him near my children ever, ever again, that he belonged in jail for child abuse and that our marriage and relationship would never be the same again!

He snickered and left the room, stating, "Suit yourself."

No, I never called the police. What a fool I was! Maybe, just maybe…oh, if only I could go back, if only…

Donald left. I don't know where he went and didn't care. The children stayed downstairs until bedtime. I went down to read, do homework, and get them cleaned up for bed. When I went in to see Kevin, he begged me to get a divorce. He told me he hated Donald. I prayed with him and each of the children as I did every night before bedtime. The others asked what they did wrong and why Donald was so mean to them. I reassured them he would never spank them again. Never!

I eventually went to bed, wondering if and when Donald would reappear and hoping he'd disappear off the face of the earth. How dare he! How dare he spank them so hard. What was he thinking? Where did this uncontrollable rage come from and why did he not apologize and why did he make it sound like it was nothing? Was there going to be more of this to come if he saw no wrong with what he did? I had seen no signs of this behaviour at all during our year of dating. How could he keep this under wraps for so long and so controlled that I didn't have the slightest inkling? Should I kick him out? How do I face others and tell them I blew it again, that I have lousy choices in men, that I'm divorcing for the second time? I prayed and prayed and prayed, and cried and cried until I finally fell asleep. I awoke hours later to hear Donald sneaking into the house and slipping under the covers. Don't touch me. Don't you dare think you can touch me!

The next morning, I arose to get ready for work and then awaken the children. Things were tense; very tense. The breakfast table was silent and nope, not one word from Donald. Not an apology, not a nothing. Unbelievable! I left for work and returned at lunch to find Donald home and wanting to talk. I told him there was nothing to talk about, that I already said he could never touch my children again and that things would never be the same between us.

He told me how unruly my children were and quoted Bible verses that the man is the head of the home and that children are to obey their parents.

I couldn't believe it and said, "Don't go quoting scripture to me. What you did was terribly wrong. The Bible doesn't give permission anywhere to beat a child!"

He calmly looked at me and reached out for my hand and said that he knew this would be hard for me but we would get through it together. He explained that my children were in desperate need of discipline and that is why God wanted two parents in a home instead of one.

I announced to him again that the children were off limits permanently to him and that if there was any disciplining to be done, it would be handled by me, and if he didn't like it, the door was open for him to leave!

You know, this is another issue we had discussed when we were dating and he totally agreed that the disciplining was up to me unless I was gone and something happened that needed an immediate reaction. I don't think we ever discussed our disciplining techniques, though. I just never dreamt in a million years that "beatings" was what his intentions were.

He had never once lost his temper or got out of control with the children while we were dating. Not once did I ever feel uncomfortable with him around the children. He never questioned their attitude toward me or his supposed lack of respect for me. My children were good; really they were! Sure they pushed my buttons once in a while, but they knew from my looks when they needed to stop their persistence and that my answer would be final.

Believe me, he dated all five of us. I couldn't afford sitters, so we didn't go out alone very often. Like I said before, he took us canoeing, came over to watch TV, went to the park with us, came over for meals, sat in church together, attended their soccer games, had fun in the water at his parents' cabin, and so on.

CHAPTER SEVENTEEN

SO WE HAD AN INTERESTING NEXT SEVERAL MONTHS. I'D COME home from work, make supper, do homework with the children, play games, watch TV, and get them ready for bed.

Donald would eat with us but not talk to the children at all. The children wanted his attention again but he would ignore them. We'd sit in the living room to watch TV and if one sat beside him, he would move to a different location. He would not answer when the children asked him questions. He would not participate in any family activities. However, he was cordial and pleasant to me. He pretended as if nothing was wrong and proceeded to be his charming self. We would talk about our daily activities but nothing deeper. Finally I questioned his mannerism with the children and how I disliked his attitude.

He told me to make up my mind and said, "First you gave permission to discipline if you weren't around when something happened, then you withdrew that offer and told me to keep my hands off, now you're back to saying you want me involved in the children's lives. Would you just make up your mind?"

Give me a break. Just because I said he couldn't discipline, that did not mean I didn't want them to be able to talk and get answers back from him. I wanted him to learn to love them and vice versa. I wanted to be a family. I did *not* want to just co-habitate!

Donald was a very cut and dry kind of guy. It was either this way or not at all, plain and simple. Donald's way or no way! To top it all off, he firmly believed his way was God's way. Forget it. There was no way I was giving permission for him to beat my children; that was not biblical. That was not going to happen.

We talked until I had to get back to work. Of course, that evening, he didn't want to talk about it. He said I had a choice to make: give him parenting permission or he wouldn't participate in the children's lives. He told me I needed counseling—that I needed to read my Bible more and that the husband was the head of the home and my role was to be submissive, that he thought I was a Christian and was shocked at this side of me, that he was disappointed in me and I had a twisted version of Christianity and twisted it to suit me, that my children were spoiled and lazy and needed a man to give them direction. I couldn't believe what I was hearing. Where was this coming from? I had thought we were on the same page. I heard him teach the Bible study, had daily conversations about our beliefs, and thought he respected me and appreciated how well-behaved my children were. Now, I was hearing a total flip-side to him. How can someone be so deceptive and so different for a whole year, and then do an about-face into someone I didn't recognize at all? How long do you have to date before you truly know someone?

Remember I told you that I saved and bought a trampoline for the children, that neighbor children came over often, and that some called me mom? Well that soon changed also. As soon as other children were in the yard, Donald would go and talk to them, ask where they live, how old they were, whether they attended the same school as my children and on and on. He said he didn't want them in our yard just to use the trampoline. If they weren't friends outside of this, they weren't allowed in the yard anymore. If they were older, they needed to leave. He was basically alienating us from everyone who used to feel comfortable at our place.

I always thought it was great having everyone at our place; at least I knew where my children were and that they weren't getting into trouble. Now no one wanted to come to our place because of Donald, and my children were no longer playing at home either. They would come up with every excuse to go to a friend's home. My girlfriends would no longer come to our house for coffee. We were all becoming very alone. Our once open, welcoming home was now a closed door to anyone we knew.

I remember having a birthday party for one of the children. The children came for supper, games, and to sleep over. Get this: Donald got up the next morning at 7 am and woke everyone up, had breakfast, and said they needed to leave now. I thought they would sleep till noon and still spend the afternoon together. Not a chance! Donald wasn't about to let the children have any fun. He got them up and pushed them to cut the lawns, shovel snow, clean house, or whatever the case may be. So birthdays and sleepovers also ceased to exist.

Then there was the cat trap. Yeah, Donald was frustrated with the smell of cat urine in our front flower bed. Yes, there was a city bylaw, but come on; these were our neighbor's cats. Anyway, he set traps and then took the cats to the SPCA and the owners would wonder what happened to them, or would have to pay to get them back, or worse yet, after a time limit, they would be put down. My children were being harassed at school dramatically about the cruelty of their so-called new dad. The school contacted Donald and asked him to come to school with a trap to explain that it didn't harm the cat and they were handled with care. This did not alleviate the bullying and abuse the children began receiving from their once-upon-a-time friends.

As for so-called Dad, that was another issue. He wanted the children to call him Dad. That would show him respect and he demanded that. To begin with they were all quite willing, however, after the first beating, there was hesitation on all their parts to address him with any kind of endearment. This later became an extreme area of contention in the home.

We got a puppy, Taffy. She was a yellow lab and a beautiful addition to our family. I was surprised Donald would even allow this. However, Donald demanded respect and obedience from her also. Often, I would see him beating her into submission. Amazingly, Taffy would cry and cry after he hit her and yet when Donald walked out the door, she would wag her tail and beg for his attention. I often saw myself in her, willing to take the abuse and still go back for his attention. How stupid was I? I can't explain why women don't leave abusive situations. I just know I've been there, done that, and saw it numerous times with victims I dealt with through my volunteering.

One day, Kevin, who would have been about thirteen, had done something wrong again. Who knows what it was this time? It was cold and snowing outside. Donald demanded an apology from Kevin and kicked him outside, with no coat, no shoes. Then Donald proceeded into the living room to joke with the other children and watch TV as if nothing was wrong.

I told him I was going to let Kevin in and he gave me a look, and said, "Don't you dare open that door."

I paced the floors and kept going to the back bedroom to peer through the window to see if he was okay. He had crawled into the dog house with Taffy to keep warm. He saw me lurching in the dark and I opened the window. He was crying and told me how cold he was. I whispered for him to pound on the living room window and say I'm sorry and beg his forgiveness. That's what Kevin did and was finally let back into the house. What mom, who loved and adored her children, would allow this kind of abuse and suffering? I'm sorry, so sorry, but I don't have an answer for you. Was I afraid of what Donald would do? Who knows? I know I would have taken a beating myself for the children, but I honestly thought he'd make me watch as he would beat them in front of me.

A few months after our wedding, there was a knock at our door. It was a sheriff serving papers to Donald in regards to Maintenance (child support to his two boys). I assumed Donald had been making regular payments, but couldn't recall seeing anything come out of our account recently.

Donald was hesitant to share the documents with me. I insisted and looked them over. He had not made payments and—get this—had no intentions of making any. He said you couldn't get blood from a stone and besides, he insisted his ex-wife was not using the money for his boys anyway.

I looked at him in total shock once again. Here he was, professing to be this outstanding Christian, following the Bible to the T, and yet saying he had no intentions of making child support payments. Who was he kidding? I don't get it. Why do some men think their child support payments shouldn't be as much as what the court orders? After all, if I had no children, I could have lived in a basement suite or much smaller house, like a one-bedroom instead of five; could have had a smaller vehicle, fewer groceries, less household gas, water, electricity bills, less furniture, no school supplies or expenses, no children's clothing, no hearing aid expenses, no other medical expenses, one dental bill instead of five, less vehicle maintenance and definitely less gas.

Good grief, men, do you think the money is supposed to all go to the children for toys and clothes? It takes a lot more than that to raise a child and I couldn't believe the man I now married took this same stand. We had discussed numerous times how Robert had not paid me and how much my children did without things because of my lack of income.

This document said Donald would be going to jail if he did not make payments and there was a court date. Donald looked directly at me and said he had no intentions of going to court and told me to ignore the documents. I insisted he had to go to court and settle on a payment arrangement. He adamantly refused and said he'd go to jail but he would not make any payments! He actually said that he always felt he should be in prison ministries! I asked him how he would be a husband to me from jail and what about our marriage and his commitment to me and the children, and he said I could handle things, and besides, I didn't want him participating in the children's lives much anyway. Unbelievable!

Well, I went to court and appeared before the judge and explained that Donald was unavailable but that we were willing to make payments. I told Donald about this. He was upset but I didn't care. I was the one who signed the checks and sent them to Maintenance. I knew prior to our marriage that he had obligations to his children and knew that would be part of our budget, however, he continued to make things overwhelmingly difficult for me.

I had no idea whatsoever that Donald was in arrears so much. Because he owned his own business, he chose to cut his wages drastically because he knew that Maintenance Enforcement would be monitoring this. He went from $27,000 annually down to $6,000 annually. I made payments of $3,290 the first year we were married and then nothing the second year because of this drastic change. Once again, the sheriff was at our door and once again Donald refused to go to court and I went on his behalf. Donald refused to increase his wages but I refused to *not* pay his children. So I told the court I would try $200 or more a month and faithfully made the payments.

As far as Donald's desire to see his children, that was a joke. He made no attempt whatsoever to contact them. He told me they knew his number and they could call him if they wanted. I told him that was unrealistic and it was up to him to build a relationship with them. I knew when their birthdays were and would buy cards, make Donald sign them, and I would attempt to mail them if he gave them to me. I would try to get him to call at least on their birthdays or Christmas. On rare occasions he would call, but I don't remember it being more than five times in nine years.

After the office was moved out of the home, I found some of the cards addressed to the children in his desk drawer—never sent. It was me who figured out when the boys would graduate and I phoned every single school in their city to ask when the graduation ceremonies were and whether they attended there. I managed to convince Donald to drive the five hours to attend the ceremonies even if he didn't make an attempt to approach the boys. At the first son's graduation, we handed a card to someone and asked them to pass it on to him. At the second son's graduation, the son came looking for us and spoke to Donald and met me. In spite of this reunion, Donald made no further attempt to contact the boys.

Five years after we got married, we had an opportunity to buy a few acres of land a few miles from town. We bought an old mobile home for $10,000 and had it moved to the property and put in water, sewer, power, septic field, etc. We attached a double, two-storey garage and put three more bedrooms and a bathroom upstairs and the garage below. Much to my dismay, when we sold the house in town, we discovered there was a lien against it for Donald's outstanding child support. What upset me also was the fact that we checked with our lawyer prior to purchasing the home as to whether a lien could be put on it, and if we should put it in my name only. We were told that if it was in both names, it couldn't be touched. So a total of $22,067 was taken from the equity in *our* home and sent to his ex-wife. That depleted our equity drastically. We decided to put the title of our new property in my name only. Why? I'm sure Donald had full intentions of not making any additional payments to his children, but from this point on, I never missed a payment; not a one. At least I could have a clear conscience even though Donald didn't. I mean, Donald didn't have a conscience!

This wasn't the only debt Donald refused to pay. It wasn't long after our marriage that we started receiving threatening calls at home and demands for payments on student loans I was totally unaware of. I found out he wasn't paying anything toward these. These loans were for attending Bible school, where he achieved his Bachelor of Religion degree. The confusing thing to me was that, once again, he had no intention whatsoever of paying these back. I have no idea where his concept of borrowing money came from. In his mind, he could just continue to borrow and not make any payments. However, for someone like me who was a fanatic about keeping payments up-to-date, and balancing to the penny every month, this was unexplainable and incomprehensible. I didn't get how he could be so rigid with his rules and laws of obeying the Bible, and yet the verses that say not to owe anyone anything didn't apply to him.

I honestly think Donald thought if he had been wronged or treated unjustly, he was getting payback by not making payments on debt. I know he thought the amount he was supposed to be paying for his two boys, $500 per month, was too much. He also was extremely upset that the Bible school refused to consider him for the ministry because of his divorce, which at the time was unacceptable in that particular denomination. Thus, he refused to continue the payments. How strange. The school had already received the money from the banks, so he wasn't punishing them in any way. And in regards to the children, somehow he thought his ex-wife didn't deserve anything, but in reality, he was hurting his children.

CHAPTER EIGHTEEN

I THOUGHT MOVING TO THE ACREAGE WAS GOING TO PULL US together as a family. We lived close to a river and coulees—deep ravines. We had checked the depth of the river and knew where the children could go and set limits, and of course we had to be with them. We would walk along the shoreline upstream a ways and wade out into the water and then lay back, allowing the current to drift us downstream. We'd have races to see who could get home first.

We went for lots of walks in the coulees and got to know and socialize with the neighbors. We had a fire pit and bought a hot tub. Hmm, this was great for me! I was a farm girl and soaked up every minute in the country. I even liked the drive home from work. It gave me a chance to collect my thoughts and be prepared to face the family and events of the evening when I'd walk through the door at home.

However, this idealistic location and fantasy was destroyed very quickly.

Donald wanted to develop the acreage and that was great by me. We had about three acres. He wanted to plant trees, put in underground sprinklers, plant a large portion to lawn, develop a three-tier fire pit area sheltered by trees, haul sand for a volleyball court, and on and on. The children were excited with us and anticipating more fun family time with way more to do than the city offered.

Once the trees were planted, however, Donald decided it was the children's job to water them, by carrying pails of water to each one. He asked Nathan and Olivia to do this on one particularly scorching summer day. They were quite young and it took both of them to carry or drag the five-gallon pail to each tree. We're talking about fifty-plus trees spread over three acres of land. Well, the children were really thinking. They connected all the garden hose they could find and timed how long it took to fill a five-gallon pail and then proceeded to lay the hose by each tree and timed it. Smart, right?

Not! Donald came home in the middle of the day to see if they were obeying him and was angry and offended to see they had used their brains to simplify the work. He punished them severely. While pulling the hose from Nathan's hands, he ripped his hands open until they bled. Then Donald told them to start all over again and do it the way he said in the first place. When I came home from work at 5:30, they were still carrying pails and continued to do so until dark. Donald would not give in and said if they would have obeyed in the first place, they'd be done by now. I remember Donald telling me how he had to water trees as a child out at the cottage and it never hurt him. I'm not sure how he could say that, considering he was still angry at his dad about it and had a strained relationship with him. Perhaps it never hurt him physically, but it certainly did mentally.

Remember I said we bought an old mobile home? Well you can't even imagine how hot this was in the summer, in the country, with no trees or shade to be found. We bought a window air conditioner. However, the children and I could not lift and install this because it was too heavy. Do you think Donald would put it in? The second year we had it, he decided the children shouldn't be sitting in the house anyway. There was lots to do outside and he refused to set it up for us. I would come home from work and be dripping wet in minutes. It was impossible to think about cooking a meal or even being hungry. The children and I would go down to the river to cool off and I'd make salads or burgers and eat outside with them. Sleeping didn't come easy either because of the heat and it certainly didn't cool off in the evenings. Donald was making it impossible to enjoy our new home.

When the children went back to school in September, it was common for us to come home to find the home ransacked. The first time it happened I went to call the police to report a break-in but Donald told me not to bother, that he had been searching for something. He had pulled and dropped the drawers in Kevin's bedroom—breaking the drawer frames. The bed was stripped. Clothes were strewn everywhere. Donald said he was looking for cigarettes and other stuff and didn't trust Kevin. He said Kevin could clean up his room by himself and he could care less how angry Kevin and I were. I would help Kevin reassemble his room, through our tears and frustration. Kevin begged me to get out of this marriage. He hated Donald and couldn't stand living with us anymore. He wanted out so badly. It seemed Kevin couldn't do or say anything right. It just came across that Donald wanted him out of the house because he believed Kevin was the cause of all our problems. Donald was trying to convince me I was a lousy mom, our children were lazy, and that things needed to change drastically.

For years, Donald had received little promotional items from the local gas station for a fill-up: things like microwave popcorn, licorice, pudding packages, etc. When he brought the pudding packages home he put them in the pantry and I assumed they were for the family and let the children take them in their lunches or for a snack after school. We learnt never to assume anything that concerns Donald. When Donald went to the pantry and they were gone, he hollered and asked who was taking *his* stuff. The following week when I went to his office, there were about forty packages of pudding in his desk drawers or under his desk, saved just for him. How could he possibly consider sharing with my children? Really? How can he be so selfish?

The children were buying some of their own special treats like ice cream and would put their name on the container in the freezer. Donald would freak out and eat it because, in his opinion, what right did they have to have their own food and yet eat ours? You've got to be kidding me! It was okay for him to bring home things we couldn't have, but not vice versa.

Donald would make popcorn, which we all know has an addictive smell and attraction to just have some. The family would watch a movie and Donald would give some to everyone except Kevin, because in his opinion, Kevin had no respect for him and broke some of the family rules. Therefore, I wouldn't eat any either and would leave the room crying. How cruel can one man be? Kevin would sit and watch the movie and be totally left out until he finally started buying his own popcorn. Guess what? The first time Kevin went to use the microwave to pop his popcorn, Donald got up halfway through the popping and threw it in the garbage. Donald informed Kevin that he didn't pay the power bill, so he couldn't use the microwave. There came a point when Kevin just stayed in his bedroom, behind closed doors, because he certainly couldn't be around Donald. The only time he was with us was when Donald went away, and we lived for those days to come more regularly.

Donald and I fought constantly. When we went up to our bedroom or after the children were all in bed, I would holler at him or try to stay calm, neither worked, and discuss how cruel he was and that he couldn't keep doing this. When we went outside I would lose it, and tell him what a bully he was and how abusive and controlling he was. He would tell me to quiet down so the neighbors wouldn't come over. I didn't care. Nothing was getting through to him. Nothing. What was it going to take?

I approached our pastor and he set up an appointment to see both of us. He listened to my concerns and all Donald said was that I wasn't willing to let him be the head of the home and that the children were unruly. The pastor started seeing us regularly to see how things were going and would give me biblical readings and assignments on submission and family things and Donald would be given assignments on grace. I would do all my homework and Donald wouldn't touch his. We'd continue to go back to counseling and I would be told things weren't as bad as I was making them out to be and that I needed to give Donald control of the family situations. I couldn't believe what I was hearing. The pastor wasn't listening, basically didn't believe me, or didn't understand verbal abuse at all.

When I was a single mom, I had practiced reading a short Bible story or a few verses to the children and then having breakfast together. However, with Donald, he would read and then ask questions and if we couldn't answer them, he'd reread it and if we still couldn't answer correctly, we wouldn't get to eat at all. We also took turns praying each day. Donald told Kevin he couldn't pray because his prayers wouldn't reach God because he was "sinning." I couldn't believe what I was hearing. This was getting way out of hand. Now we were being spiritually abused also; so much so, that our basic necessities were being withheld from us.

We bought a satellite dish for our television. We only had one receiver, so whatever was being watched on one television, the second one had to be the same. The main receiver was upstairs in our bedroom. The children and I could be watching a movie, could be more than halfway through it, and if Donald so chose, he'd go up to our bedroom and change the channel to some stupid show none of us wanted—and nothing he would normally watch either. He would do this just to bully and control us. If he didn't want the children watching television for some reason—or me, for that matter—he just changed channels.

I would go up and insist he change the channel back until our show was over and he would look at me defiantly and refuse. It was like having another rebellious teenager in the house, except this one had total control. The only time we really enjoyed watching a program, or doing anything, was when Donald was away. If only those times would have come more often! Oh, and get this, on numerous occasions Donald would call the satellite company and disconnect the dish entirely so that we had no reception at all. The stupid thing was that I bought the dish with my money, and the bill of sale was in my name, but he set it up and got the code. When I'd call in to reactivate it, they wouldn't let me because he told them *he* was the only one allowed to make changes to the account.

Kevin got a part-time job and Donald insisted he start paying rent to us. Donald felt half of his income should go to us, even if he was still under eighteen and attending school. I really thought Donald's goal would be to save this and later give it back to Kevin for the purchase of a vehicle or something, but no, Donald spent the money himself. It wasn't used for household expenses or anything, just pocketed by Donald. We had a low income and I felt that if the children could work and still keep up their grades, they deserved their own money for the extras they wanted, like school ski trips, youth events, movies, etc. Donald basically shut down any motivation they would have to work by stripping them of their pride and their money. Eventually I insisted that Kevin pay me directly and I would keep the money and use it for expenses at home.

Donald had purchased an extra computer so that I could do some of his business stuff at home instead of always going back into town at nights to work. However, the children also started using the computer for essays and different things at school. Donald never told me or the children it wasn't for personal use. Yeah, well, we would come home after work and school to find the computer gone. Donald would come home in the middle of the day, pack it up, and take it to work and set it on the floor. Not because we needed a second one at work, but because he didn't want the children to have any use of it. It was ridiculous. Then, when he felt like it, he would bring the computer home again because I did all the bookkeeping and I was exhausted going back to town in the evenings. Several times, the children had documents they had spent hours working on for school assignments but hadn't completed yet. Again the computer would disappear. He would refuse to bring the computer back for them to print it off. He just did *not* want the children to have any small pleasures. He made our life a living chaos!

As I mentioned earlier, we bought a hot tub (with loan payments) thinking it would be great out in the country and how much the children would enjoy it. When things were going good, the children and I got to enjoy it every night. Once again, Donald took control. Soon the hot tub became off-limits to all the children. Donald just didn't feel they deserved it. Go figure. One more thing taken away!

I had also talked with Donald about putting in a sand volleyball court for the children. One day we were walking by the river and commented on the mounds of beautiful sand that washed in. Donald said he'd haul it to the yard for the volleyball court. So the fun began. Donald ended up loading the sand, plus the dirt and twigs and junk with it. Then he built a huge strainer and insisted the children take shovel after shovel and sift it and shovel it onto the cleared area for the volleyball court. He sure believed in pushing them to their limits if they wanted any kind of fun at all. It took that whole spring and summer before they had sifted it all, and he refused to help because it was for them, not him. When it was completed, we bought a net, set it up, and then basically looked at it. They weren't allowed to have parties. We had no friends left. Logan, Nathan, Olivia, and I would play occasionally but it was a waste.

CHAPTER NINETEEN

MY NIECE WAS GRADUATING AND I WAS INVITED TO ATTEND HER graduation, along with Kevin. Kevin would not go if Donald was going. That left me in a dilemma. It was mandatory for Kevin to attend. They were way too close for him not to be there for her. I had *never* missed their family grads! Donald told me to make a choice. I didn't go the grad. I hurt my niece and brother and sister-in-law deeply.

Shortly after we moved out to the acreage, I decided to go to a Ladies Retreat for a weekend about four hours away from home. Yes, I left Donald alone with the children. Things were good before I left, or so I thought. However, when I called home the first night, I asked to talk to the children and Donald told me he had kicked Kevin out. He had no idea where he was and it was snowing and cold. I called my brother and his wife and he was at their place in town. I talked to Kevin and he said Donald dumped his backpack in search of whatever again. Kevin said he blew up at him and Donald kicked him out. Kevin had no coat and we lived thirteen kilometres from town. He started walking and supposedly called from a neighbor's or somehow got a ride to town. He was not going back home until I returned. I had no way to get home immediately, because we had travelled on a chartered bus. My weekend was ruined, of course, and once again Kevin had no one to care for him.

There was a psychologist at this retreat, as the guest speaker. I asked if I could speak with her in private. I told her about our home situation and how Christian counselors told me I should be submissive and that we were not being abused. I told her I couldn't live like this anymore and didn't know the difference between abuse and biblical submission. In the courses I took with Victims Assistance, I had been told to go with my gut, that it is usually 95% correct. Why had I been feeling like getting out for so long already but no one was advising me to do so? Could I have been that wrong? Was everything the children's and my fault?

She sat and talked with me extensively and said she'd really like to meet with the whole family on a weekend. She lived three hours from our home, but I told her we could come and we did. She told Donald that he and Kevin had to find a way to get along and talked to them for quite a while. I honestly thought she gave them positive suggestions and I truly thought we were heading in the right direction finally. The three of us talked the whole way home and appeared to be coming up with solutions and compromises to situations.

The peace lasted less than a week.

Kevin finally moved out, two months prior to his grade twelve graduation. He literally lived on the streets and still had enough guts to finish school and graduate. He was determined not to go to his grad at all and wouldn't even reconsider if Donald wouldn't be there. I finally convinced Kevin to at least participate in the grad ceremonies and he said he would, and I promised Donald wouldn't be there. I invited about twenty friends and relatives to meet at a restaurant after to celebrate. I was so very proud of him. Kevin had struggled so much and yet had the determination and willpower to get his grade twelve. Wow!

Needless to say, when I returned home that night, I was given the cold shoulder and Donald was up to his usual "not talking to me" stage. I should have been used to this already. He could go days, weeks, months without saying a word to anyone in the house.

Kevin was still working at the restaurant. He lived with my brother for a while, but things became complicated and he was no longer there. I remember the cold weather coming that fall and Kevin was living in a tent. I would take food to him and leave it outside his tent and it would be frozen by the time he'd get home, but he would try to reheat it over a campfire. The snow started flying and it was getting colder and colder.

Kevin showed up at my office. His lips were blue. He was whispering when he first came in. He looked at me and asked why I was choosing

Donald over my own flesh and blood. I wondered the same thing. He wanted to come home so badly, but knew Donald wouldn't let him. He was cold and hungry and had no place to go. Donald had told me over and over that I needed to stand up and show "tough love" to Kevin and that he could come home if he would follow Donald's rules. Kevin had refused. Soon Kevin's voice began to escalate. He started hollering and swearing and proceeded to call me every name in the book, from "whore" to "slut" to "useless" to "bitch." Finally, one of my co-workers came and removed him out the back door of the office.

A few days later he showed up again. He said sorry and asked if he could just sit in the van to warm up. I would start the van and let him sleep in it, out in the parking lot, just so he had a warm place to be. I would bring food from home so he could eat in the van also. I don't know where he went at nights. It was impossible for me to sleep. My nights were spent praying and praying for his safety and for a change of heart from him and Donald. Over and over I'd pray for a miracle. That's what it would take, believe me! It was a long time later that I found out Kevin was breaking in to my brother's business and going up to the attic and sleeping at nights and leaving early in the mornings so he wouldn't be caught. How awful; no place to go. I can't even begin to imagine the torment and pain he must have been in emotionally.

I can only imagine what you're thinking right now. What mother could possibly turn her back on her own son? Believe me, you can't possibly imagine what I was going through. You really don't know unless you've been through it yourself. I used to get ticked off when I would go out with the police and discuss domestic dispute issues as part of my volunteer work with Victims Assistance. The police also wondered why women were so stuck as to stay in the home and take the abuse instead of getting out. It's not because I wasn't competent enough to live on my own, because believe me, I was overly independent and definitely didn't need a man to take care of me.

It was the fear—the absolute terror of wondering what would happen to me or the children if I left. I sincerely didn't care if Donald killed me; after all, it would take me out of this misery. However, I didn't want any harm to come to my children. I was petrified he would do something to them. Plus, he told me over and over what an incompetent mother I was and that I'd lose all my children if I didn't wise-up. He'd quote scripture to me over and over and try to point out that he was supposed to be the head of the home and that children were to obey their parents.

I remember the boys asking me if they could just retaliate and hit back. I warned them against that. I told them if they ever lost control and hit him first, he would use that against them and kick them out and press charges against them. However, if he hit first, I told them to do whatever it took to protect themselves. There were times Donald would be so angry and he would almost be nose to nose with one of the boys and they would back down the hallway until their back was against a bedroom wall. He pushed them to the extremes and I have no idea how they had enough control to not punch his lights out.

I moved into Kevin's bedroom after he moved out. I needed time to think, time to put things into perspective, time to make some decisions, time for the Lord and me.

Several years prior this, I had started a prayer book. I read my Bible every day and I would write in a notebook things to pray for in our family, things at work, things people told me they were concerned about, people sick, financial stress for people, teenage issues of friends, etc. You name it, I prayed for it. God wasn't someone I went to once a day. Yes, I set aside special time in the morning for Him and me, but I prayed all day. God was, and still is, my best friend. I talk to Him whether I'm going for a walk, driving the car, sitting at my desk, whatever. No, I don't close my eyes and get on my knees every time. I say a quick sentence prayer, knowing He hears me, and carry on.

The prayer book helped me not to forget and I would often look back and see how God was answering prayer. I would go back several pages and see how time after time things worked out for people I was praying for, and how gracious God was in circumstances. However, I also noted how desperate I was. I still have the prayer book from that time period. Early in our marriage I wrote how empty, defeated, worthless, abused, trapped, and rejected I felt, and what a lousy mom I was. The word "help" is in it numerous times.

It's strange looking back on it. One day I would write about my desperation and a week later I was writing how content and happy I was and thanking God for bringing me through another situation. This goes on for years in my prayer book. I never realized how bad it was, until I looked back on it now—twelve years later. I was begging God for a way out. Begging!

The book also says how loving Donald is. What a twist. How can one be so mean and yet be so loving? Was I so desperate for touch and affection that it blinded me so severely to the abuse in our home? The thing is, the pastor and other Christian counselors never called it abuse. They never used that word: abuse! Why? So how could I help but feel the problem was all me and the children? No one affirmed my feelings. No one told me I was okay. No one acknowledged that what was going on was wrong. No one ever reprimanded Donald. Oh, I wished he would have just beaten me up and given me bruises or a black eye so I could run and shout, "See, I'm not lying. This is what he's doing to us!" How does one ever prove mental abuse?

CHAPTER TWENTY

DONALD LEFT US AT CHRISTMAS TIME. I ASKED KEVIN TO COME home for Christmas and Donald said he wouldn't be there if Kevin was. For once I stuck to my convictions and said that would have to be his choice but Kevin was coming home. (Yeah, I did one thing right.) We were supposed to be going to Donald's side of the family that year. I came home the day before the holidays to find a note from him stating he felt we'd enjoy our Christmas better without him, and thus he wouldn't be around.

I was so tempted to go to his parents without him. Basically, he was stripping us of all our plans and fun again. Forbid it, if the children should ever be allowed to have a good time! So now what? I had no turkey, no baking, nothing. I wasn't planning on being at home. Oh well. We made the best of it. We played games, watched movies, and curled up together and were happy. Yes, happy without the fights, confrontations, hiding, and wondering when or how Donald would blow up at Kevin or anyone else.

After Kevin left, Donald amazingly reappeared as if nothing had happened or changed. He refused to discuss it and when I attempted to bring it up, he told me to get over it! Oh, and all Donald's presents remained unopened for a long time. The children had gone out of their way to buy him special things and paid attention to what he enjoyed and he refused to open them. Eventually, when he did open them, weeks and weeks later, they went on a shelf and were never touched.

Somehow, after Christmas, Donald and I started talking again. Donald was cordial to the kids again. Things were almost peaceful and happy. We shared a bedroom again.

Shortly after Kevin left, Donald bought a different vehicle. However, it only had room for five passengers. Of course he never showed it to me in advance, nor did he ask my opinion. I asked him why he would choose a vehicle that only sat five because there were six of us. He said Kevin moved out and wasn't welcome.

My mom became extremely ill and we were told she probably would not make it. My parents live six hours away. Kevin wanted to come with us to see her, however there was no room for him. This was totally intentional on Donald's part. He did not want Kevin with us any longer.

The other thing about this stupid, shiny, new vehicle was that it had leather seats. The front seats were heated but the back ones weren't. Donald would turn the heat down and sometimes off because he was plenty warm enough with the seat heater on. The children were freezing in the back and Donald refused to turn the heat up. I took off my coat and laid it over them. They complained of their feet freezing but Donald didn't care. Then they would ask to change radio stations or to turn it up and he would turn it to some opera channel or something stupid that none of us liked. I cringe as I sit here reminiscing about how evil and cruel Donald was to us. Even more so, I hate what I did to my children by not leaving. I hate that I believed so strongly in my vows, in commitment, in marriage, that I risked my children for it. I hate that I didn't get out sooner and didn't protect them. I hate what he did to us.

Since Donald had always said Kevin was the disobedient and defiant troublemaker in our home, now that my oldest son had moved out our problems should have all be gone, right? Well, the truth was soon to be shown.

One day, the children arrived home from the bus and I received a panicked phone call at work from Logan. His computer wasn't working. Logan said he pulled on the cords and they were cut. I couldn't believe what I was hearing. Logan crawled under the mobile home and everything was cut. We already knew Donald was the culprit.

Logan was in grade twelve and working hard to keep up his grades, worked part-time, and took extra computer courses online so he'd have enough credits to graduate. Logan had bought his own computer and because we were in the country, we could only use dial-up for internet. Donald did not want the internet used while we were awake, in case there was a business call or a family emergency. Logan honored that, so much so that he would come home and eat, then sleep for several hours, then set his alarm for midnight and do his online courses while we slept.

Well, of course, this still wasn't good enough for Donald. Donald came home during the day and disconnected everything on his computer. When I came home and approached Donald about this, he said Logan needed a life, he was a computer fanatic and needed more in his life. What a joke! Logan had a part-time job, was involved in sports, involved in youth at the church—what more did Donald want?

Logan told me he was moving out. I couldn't believe what I was hearing. Logan was the one who went out of his way to defend Donald. He was the one who had appeared to find no wrong with what Donald was doing to Kevin. He was the one who admired and respected Donald for his faith and knowledge in God. Now he was walking out too? I was about to lose my second son. The pain was overwhelming! My emotions were torn and my insides felt like they were being ripped out again. How much more could we take? Logan had no idea where he would go—just away from here.

In the meantime, I had disclosed what was happening at home to a girlfriend. She asked if Logan could housesit for her while she was planning to be away for six weeks. I thought she was insane. Logan was a seventeen-year-old boy in his last month of grade twelve. How could she possibly trust him to not have a party, wreck the house, or whatever?

She told me she trusted him implicitly and to give it some thought. I approached Logan with her offer and he couldn't believe it. He jumped at the offer and said he'd keep the house spotless, water and cut the lawn, and do whatever she wanted for the six weeks.

So Logan moved out. Logan studied, kept up his grades, wrote his finals, and graduated. He worked for the remainder of the six weeks during her absence and then decided to return home for the few remaining weeks prior to leaving for Bible school. It was a struggle for him to be home again, but he basically worked and stayed in his room in the evenings, unless Donald was away; then he'd join the rest of us.

After Logan left, I moved into his bedroom. I begged Donald to move out. He refused. We never spoke at all. He still had meals with us where no one said a word. When he walked in the house, we all dispersed into hiding and when he left there was laughter, fun, and relaxation. Then he would enter and the silence would begin again.

During this separation, Donald started coming into my bedroom in the middle of the night. He'd kneel by my bed, kiss me, and then leave. Then he'd come back another night and slip his hands under the covers and touch me and I'd tell him to get lost and he'd leave. He continued this night after night after night. I began locking my door and he'd come and try to open the door and stomp away.

Donald hated when I drove Nathan to work or when I had to go into town later in the evening to pick Nathan up. Donald wanted the children to work, but he didn't like that we needed to drive them. He was frustrated when I was so exhausted and still had to go and get them. He didn't want me running to town to take them to youth at church, either.

Of course, Donald wouldn't help with parenting. I was still a single mom. He wanted them to be Christians but wanted no part of being a parent and a good role model. If there was a youth event and they were having a bike trip, Donald told me he didn't want me doing all the running and taking the bikes to town. He said the children could bike there if they really wanted to go. Give me a break! We were thirteen kilometers from town. How were they supposed to get home from school, bike to town, bike during the youth event, and then bike home again? It was an impossibility! I talked to Nathan and Olivia and told them to load the bikes very, very quietly while I was doing dishes and Donald was reading the paper after supper. I had purposely backed into the garage. After the dishes were done, I slipped outside, pulling the door closed silently, and pushed the truck down the driveway, so Donald wouldn't hear the engine and then started it and sped off for town. How ridiculous is that? I knew I'd get the third degree when I got home, but I didn't care!

Soon, Christmas was coming again. What would this year be like? It was getting to the point that both the children and I dreaded it. We had no idea whether Donald would walk out and leave us alone again or whether he would even be with us. Of course, we all knew it probably depended on whether Kevin or Logan would come home. Christmas came and Donald didn't join us again. He slept at the shop. Fine! We had more fun without him anyway. We enjoyed every minute of our holiday time together with just the kids and me and wished he wouldn't come home at all!

CHAPTER TWENTY-ONE

GUESS WHAT? THE WRITING WAS ON THE WALL. WE ALL FEARED AND knew the inevitable would happen to the next child. Nathan loved tinkering with mechanics of some sort. He had been working part-time and purchased a cheap dirt bike to get back and forth to the city. One evening he dismantled it and had lots and lots of parts in a pail in the corner of the garage. He was waiting for a part in order to reassemble it.

Donald came home and decided, for some unknown reason, that he didn't want his parts in the garage and proceeded to empty the pail outside, down the hillside, scattering the tiny pieces everywhere. Nathan came home from school and was devastated to find what Donald had done. He was crying when I came home from work. It was to the point that none of us even asked Donald "Why" anymore, because he didn't need a reason. It was just because he was mean and cruel to all of us. Nathan, Olivia, and I spent hours and hours scouring through the tall grass and hillside looking for nuts, bolts, and tiny parts to the dirt bike. We got some cardboard and laid it on the carpet in Nathan's room and carried everything upstairs into his bedroom. Donald told us at supper that the garage was for his vehicles and not for everyone's junk.

Nathan saved money and bought a tent so he could sleep in the yard and get away from everything, too. He wanted to have some fun. He asked if he could invite friends over and I had absolutely no problem with having other friends over on occasion. Donald asked him to be sure and move the tent each morning so that it wouldn't kill the lawn. Nathan was faithful each morning and moved it to a spot in the yard where no grass had been planted. Once again, that wasn't good enough for Donald. It seemed he just didn't want us to have any kind of fun or enjoyment in life whatsoever!

Donald came home one extremely windy day and proceeded to take all the pegs out of the tent. When Nathan came home from school, the tent was gone. He was frantic and searched for it in the coulee. It was ripped to shreds! The men who worked for Donald's company told me Donald had been at coffee that day joking about what he had done. One of the other contractors asked him why, and Donald said it was to teach him a lesson of some sort.

Nathan told me this was it: he was moving. He couldn't stand living here anymore and couldn't figure out why I was willing to lose three sons and still stay. He was done! I don't know where he went or how he got to town. The Sunday school picnic was the next day. I was an emotional wreck! I managed to contact Nathan and begged him to come home. I begged him to hang in there with me! Nathan came home that night.

Once again I asked Donald for a separation. He finally moved downstairs. That's as much of a separation as I could get from him. The bedroom door was locked when I crawled into bed each night, but he would unlock it with a nail and I'd awaken and hear him breathing quietly on the floor by the bed. I remember pretending I was sleeping and hoping and praying he would leave. He would put his hand under the covers and try to touch me and I would conveniently roll over, in hopes he would think I was waking up and would leave. One night, he kept groping for me. I finally sat up and told him to get out of there. I told him we were done and to get out right now. He got up and slammed the door and left. After that, I lay there, heart pounding, wondering when he'd come back. I couldn't sleep. I prayed. How much were Nathan and Olivia hearing in the two bedrooms across the hall? How long could I remain quiet without scaring them or have them walk in on something?

Logan started dating Rebecca while at Bible school. He had brought her home, along with another friend, once before, but they hadn't started dating at that point. This time it was Thanksgiving and I called and asked Kevin if he'd come and join us.

I knew Donald wouldn't appreciate having Kevin there, but I told him I invited him and wanted Kevin to see Logan and meet Rebecca. It was quite a warm day and with the turkey cooking, the mobile home was overly hot. I knew Donald didn't approve nor accept Kevin's style of music and Kevin was well aware of that also. Kevin graciously wore a long-sleeved shirt over his Pennywise (a band) t-shirt.

We sat down to enjoy a good Thanksgiving meal and have good conversation and have a chance to get better acquainted with Rebecca. When I got up to get the dessert, Kevin excused himself and said he was way too hot. He came back with just his t-shirt on and sat down.

Donald took one look at him and his t-shirt and didn't think twice about having company there. He just blurted out, as usual, and told Kevin to either put his other shirt back on or leave. I couldn't believe what I was hearing again. Give me a break! It's just a t-shirt! Couldn't we just have one meal without some sort of confrontation from Donald? Couldn't he just once overlook and accept Kevin for who he was? Couldn't he just keep his thoughts to himself and suck it up? And what was Rebecca thinking?

So, once again, Kevin was very polite and excused himself and walked outside. I went running after him. He just said to let it go and gave me a hug and thanked me for the meal. He got in his vehicle and drove off. I walked back into the house in tears, refusing to cause another scene in front of Rebecca, biting my tongue, and proceeded to hand out the dessert. We sat in silence. Another day ruined by Donald. How much longer should I stay in this relationship and let him torment us? How many more times would Donald embarrass and humiliate me?

Donald and I still were not sleeping together. We were apart for over three months. Suddenly, out of the blue, he started talking more to me and things actually seemed cordial and almost bearable. Then I found out my parents were planning to come and spend Christmas with us. I hadn't told anyone we were separated. Donald was sending me cards and was joking with Nathan and Olivia and it almost seemed pleasant in our home again. Yes, the honeymoon was beginning again and I fell under his spell and finally moved back into our bedroom.

You may be wondering why I went back. In fact, why do women stay or quite often go back to the abuser? I really don't have an answer for you. I told you before I was independent and didn't count on, or rely on Donald. However, Donald was good at romancing. He knew all the right words to say. He knew how to push my buttons, to charm me, to make me feel beautiful and wanted. He went overboard in meeting those needs. *And* I knew that divorce was wrong and wanted so badly to not end another marriage.

Christmas came and went and no one suspected how strained our relationship was. Donald was cordial and pleasant to everyone and made our home and marriage appear perfectly normal to everyone. It was actually an enjoyable Christmas for a change.

Donald was president of the contractor's association and we were supposed to be going to Mexico right after Christmas—totally paid for. I told him to book for himself and that I wouldn't be attending. He said he was booking for both of us in hopes I would change my mind. I told him it would never happen. Of course, Donald was up to his honeymoon tricks again. He'd buy flowers and send them to my office. He'd send cards. He'd write love letters and leave them on my bed. We'd come home to a cooked meal and he was joking and interacting with the children. Of course, he'd leave letters quoting verse after verse from the Bible telling me how I was to be submissive and love my husband, that divorce was absolutely wrong and not an option.

We began talking again. Eventually holding hands began again and the whole dating game. I fell right back into the trap again. I wanted it to work. I really did. I really wanted to believe he had changed; that maybe he finally understood. How stupid, gullible, desperate could I possibly be? How pathetic I was! How pathetic!

Once again, he whittled his way back into my heart and it was only two weeks away from the Mexico holiday. I agreed to go. Minutes before we left, with me waiting in the vehicle, Donald drove the other truck into the double garage and parked it in the middle and took the keys with him. I asked what he was doing. It was 40 below and snowing so much. We were going to be gone a week and I told the children they could park the car in the garage while we were gone. Oh,

I get it. Donald's up to his old tricks again. If he parked the one vehicle in the middle, then there would be no room for the car. How could he possibly let the children park in the garage and have that convenience while we were gone? That would be way above any generosity Donald could possibly have.

Donald got back into our vehicle and I asked what was wrong with him. He never said a word. I told him to stop the vehicle and let me out. He kept driving. I went to open the door and he stepped on the gas. He told me to not be so stupid; to sit back and look forward to an exciting week in Mexico. It was an awful week. I did not enjoy it at all. I made the best of it that I could, but told him over and over that this was the last trip we'd ever go on and that I sincerely meant it this time.

When we got home from Mexico I insisted it was over. I begged Donald to move out or the kids and I would. However, I told him it wasn't fair for three of us to move and that it should be him and not us.

He just looked at me in disbelief and told me I needed to stop threatening separation and make up my mind to be committed to the marriage. He told me how disappointed he was in me and that he'd thought I was a Christian. If I was truly a Christian, I would be committed to the marriage and our vows.

That was the hardest part about this whole thing. I was a Christian. I believed in God with all my heart. I prayed and prayed and prayed. I begged God to change Donald. I begged God to change me. I begged God to help me be a better mom, a better wife, a better everything. I felt so useless. I felt everything was my fault. After all, I had sought out numerous counselors (Christian counselors) and told them what was going on in our home. No one called it abuse. No one suggested I leave. I was constantly reminded "for better or worse." I felt obligated to stay in spite of how bad it was.

There must be verses in the Bible somewhere that would tell me how to survive this lifestyle or give me permission to leave. I searched and read and searched and read. I bought book after book. I sought out counselor after counselor; all for nothing. However, I did go to one counselor who was not from the church. When I explained to him some of the events happening in our home, he told me I was an abuser.

I couldn't believe what I was hearing. What do you mean, I'm an abuser?

He explained that if I remained in the home or didn't force Donald to leave, I was a passive abuser. In other words, by "not protecting the children," I was just as much an abuser as Donald was! I was horrified at this thought. The counselor told me if I didn't change the situation immediately, he would be forced to report it to Social Services and I would lose custody of the kids.

I went home and insisted that Donald leave. This time he moved out of our bedroom and into one of the other bedrooms downstairs in the mobile. This was as far a move as he was going to make. Really? How was this going to protect the children? He promised to not be around while the children were awake.

One Sunday afternoon while the children were gone, I lay down for a nap, locked the door, and suddenly Donald appeared in the bedroom. How did he get in? I asked him to leave. He wouldn't. He came over to the bed and lay on top of me. He would not get off. Donald was not a small man. He was well over 200 pounds. This was around 1:00 pm. I was crying and crying and felt him go limp. He was sleeping with his dead weight on me. I couldn't breathe. I was hurting so much and crying and screaming but he slept on. I thought my ribs were broken. I thought I was going to suffocate or die with his weight on me!

He finally got up—around 5 pm. The next morning before leaving for work, I told him how angry I was with him and how much he hurt me. He came and grabbed me and almost squeezed the breath out of me again and said it was his only way of showing how much he loved and missed me. When he finally let go, I shoved him away and screamed that this wasn't love!

While I was at work that next day, I remembered Donald telling me years earlier that I was welcome to read the court cases between him and his ex-wife, but that none of it was true and just to see how vindictive and how much of a liar his first wife was.

When I went to bed that night, I locked our bedroom door as usual and then proceeded into our closet and closed the door and turned on the light. I reached up onto one of the top shelves and pulled out the box from his first marriage. I sat on the floor and began reading the court transcripts. Oh my gosh! History was repeating itself. I read, in horror and disgust, of how he threw and broke things. I read of how he wanted to stick pop bottles up his wife. I read of how he laid on her for hours and hours, until she couldn't breathe.

Why didn't I read this when we first met? Why was I so sure I had overturned every stone in regards to getting remarried but I didn't check this out? I read through everything and snuck back into bed. I finally fell asleep for an hour or so before the alarm went off.

Get this! When I got ready for bed the following night, I was putting things away in the closet and noticed the box from the prior night missing. I moved things around on the shelves and it was nowhere to be found. Why would it disappear the night after I got it out and read everything? How could Donald possibly know I was in the closet that night? The closet door was closed and the bedroom door was locked and he was down in the mobile. This was totally freaking me out. Did he have a camera in our room or what? Let me think about this. He had come in that Sunday afternoon when I locked the door. Had he broken in again that night and found out I wasn't in bed? He must have! How else would he know I was in the closet?

CHAPTER TWENTY-TWO

LOGAN WAS MOVING HOME IN MAY—FOR THE SUMMER—TO WORK and his wedding was set for August. How could I possibly hang on till then? I didn't want to ruin the wedding. I knew how much Donald's side of the family had come to mean to all of us. I knew if I left Donald, they wouldn't come to the wedding. I didn't want to ruin that for Logan.

Donald and I started sharing the same bedroom again—not a marriage—just a bedroom! I told him to keep his hands off me; this was only 'till after the wedding and that we were done and that I was leaving after the wedding. I told him I was looking for a place and would be gone before school started.

Things became unbearable in our bedroom. Donald was waking every night and would fondle me for hours and hours, hoping for a response. Eventually he would give up and roll over and go to sleep. As time went by, he was becoming more aggressive. His fondling became more intrusive, invasive, and harsher. It would last for over two hours every night! The whole time I would lay there and not move a muscle—too scared to tell him to stop—but my heart would pound and I'd grit my teeth wishing and praying he'd go away. He'd finally give up. He knew I was crying and he knew he was forcing himself on me!

This went on for more than a month. I wasn't getting more than an hour or two of sleep every night! There were days I could hardly walk. I was passing blood and it hurt so much to urinate. I finally rolled over one night and thought maybe, just maybe, if I give in and give him what he wants, he'll leave me alone for a while. However, when I proceeded to make a move for him he shoved me off and ran into the bathroom and slammed the door. What's up with that? Oh, I get it. He wants to be in control. It's all about control and always has been. I rolled over, heart pounding and tried desperately to get some sleep. He never came back for quite a while but when he did, he laid on the edge of his side of the bed and finally fell asleep.

Shortly after, he had his way of paying me back for not giving in to him sexually. He came home and took the truck I was using to town. Hours later he walked back in the yard—without the truck. I asked what happened to the truck and he said he left it at the shop and felt we couldn't afford it and walked home—thirteen kilometres! What? All he was doing was punishing me. This was ridiculous! The keys were hidden. Now I was down to one vehicle again for the kids and me to share. Once again I'd be the one driving Nathan to and from work, sports, youth, and whatever. So be it! He wins again! The truck sat at the shop for over a year—never moved. We made payments on it and it never moved!

Donald didn't stop groping and fondling me. He never gave up—night after night after night.

I began looking for a place to live. What could I afford? Not much! I needed three bedrooms at least—one for me, one for Olivia, and one for Nathan. I decided to look for something effective September 1. The wedding would be over and I wouldn't need to think of a room for Logan too. The school year would be starting and we could look for something close to the school Nathan would attend. However, Olivia still wanted to attend the country school, so I was going to have to drive her to and from school every day.

I started counseling again, this time to discuss parenting skills. I was having more and more issues with Olivia. Of course our marriage came into the conversation. The counsellor asked me why I couldn't say "no" when Donald was crossing the line and raping me. Why was I letting him do this to me? Just try using the word "no." Just try it, Joy!

So, that night, it was after midnight when Donald started fondling me.

I told him to stop.

He continued.

I said, "NO, Donald, stop it! Just stop this all—just quit!"

He asked "Stop what?"

I told him, "Stop touching me, holding me, fondling me—just LEAVE ME ALONE!"

He proceeded to tell me that he was my husband and he could do whatever he wanted and I was to be submissive. He told me I was not a Christian, not obedient to the Bible, not going to Heaven. He was mad, but rolled over to sleep.

The next morning, Donald met me as I was coming out of the shower and began touching and caressing me. Once again I told him to stop! He grinned and walked away.

The following night, Donald woke me after midnight—no fondling, just rolled me over on my back and raped me. It only lasted a few minutes, but I almost thought this was better than what had been happening the past three months! I thought I could survive this if it was only ten minutes and I could sleep again. I felt so invaded, used, dirty, angry—but kept thinking only ten minutes was *great* compared to two hours.

A couple nights later, I was awoken by Donald rolling me over on my stomach and proceeding to rape me. It went on for thirty minutes or more—seemed like forever. He kept saying how beautiful I was, how he loved me, how he couldn't resist me, how he couldn't control himself. He was so harsh with his movements. My head was buried in my pillow and I was crying, with my mouth open into the pillow, hoping he wouldn't hear me—scared he'd get angrier if I wasn't enjoying it. I was motionless. He just kept on and on and on. I felt so defiled, so ugly, so angry! I gritted my teeth and begged God to end it already! He finally got off me. I ran to the bathroom and sobbed and sobbed and curled into a ball. I started dozing off on the bathroom floor and wondered if I could dare go back to bed. Would he be asleep or not?

I went to my counselor again. She asked me why I didn't say no. Why did I continue to let Donald have control? Why did I let him do this?

That night Donald yanked me from my side to my back and started to try to get on top of me. I said, "No!" and pulled my knees up to stop him. He tried to straddle his leg between mine and I began hitting his back and saying "No!"

He kept trying and I knew I didn't have the strength to keep this up. Finally I started screaming at the top of my lungs for him to stop and get off and he gave in and rolled over. I was thinking, "Woohoo! Saying no and screaming worked!" Why oh why didn't I do this before? Why am I so scared of this man? Why not let the kids come in? Perhaps this would stop Donald completely!

The following morning, unbelievably, I was coming out of the shower, and he actually had the audacity to come behind me to snuggle and caress me. Really? Really? What's it going to take to get through to this man? I am *not* his property!

The next night Donald woke me after midnight and said we needed to talk. I told him we need help and that we can't do this alone.

He started hollering at me and sassing, "Oh yes. Joy has all the answers. She knows it all." Donald woke me up four or five nights in a row to start a discussion about the same thing. There were no resolutions; no answers. We could not do this alone! I was so sleep deprived! First sexually assaulting me by fondling evasively, then rape, now conversation. Who could predict what would be next?

I asked Donald to move out—permanently. I told him we were done, totally done! I told him I did not want him there when I returned in the evening.

I went to a lawyer. I asked for a restraining order. I handed the lawyer notes I had taken the past few days which detailed the past couple months and highlighted incidents over the years. I was told a restraining order was quicker to obtain and would grant more protection if it was filed along with divorce papers. I had no intentions of filing for a divorce yet—just wanted to get him off the acreage, out of the house, out of the bed. I wanted it to stop! Please stop! I finally told the lawyer to do whatever it takes. I told the lawyer I still wanted to see Donald, for counseling or whatever, but I didn't want him allowed on our property at all.

These are a few of the points the lawyer wrote in the divorce papers and he also included my entire document describing in detail things that had been happening:

#11 It doesn't matter how many times I would confront the Defendant on his physical and sexual conduct toward me because he refuses to acknowledge that he is doing anything wrong and he doesn't appreciate the incredible fear that I live with when he is around.

#12. Lately, over the last three months, his conduct has become increasingly sporadic such that one moment he will be physically abusive toward the children or physically abusive and sexually abusive toward myself and then the next moment he will act as if nothing has happened. I am at a complete loss to understand why the Defendant behaves as he does but after almost 10 years of marriage I cannot take any more.

#13. As I have indicated in my diary in Exhibit "B," my son Logan who no longer lives with the Defendant and myself is getting married at the end of August, 2001. My son, Logan, does not realize the extent to which I have been abused by the Defendant. However, this being said, Logan has acquired many friends among the Defendant's family and accordingly I am under a great deal of pressure not to take any actions against the Defendant for fear that it may have consequences regarding my son's wedding. Unfortunately, I know that I cannot handle going another month residing with the Defendant and I am tired of living in fear. I can only hope that these actions that I have taken will not negatively impact my son's wedding at the end of August, 2001. I have reached the end of my rope and I need to do something now in order to preserve my sanity and particularly the safety of my children.

#14. I believe it is in the best interest of my children that I be granted by the Courts a Matrimonial Home Possession Order and a further Restraining Order that will prevent the Defendant from attending the matrimonial home until such time that I and my children can feel safe. My biggest concern is the Defendant attending our home and engaging in verbally and physically abusive behavior toward the children and ongoing sexual abuse toward me.

The lawyer asked if any of the children would verify my accusations to make my plea to the judge stronger.

I contacted Kevin and told him I had been to a lawyer for a restraining order. I asked Kevin if he would mind writing something so that the judge would know from a second person how bad things were at our house. I hated involving the kids, but the lawyer said this would make our case stronger.

Kevin jumped at the opportunity to help. This is what Kevin wrote.

I, Kevin Parson, would be very pleased if the legal system could work for me, and remove one Donald Stever from my life. In the past ten years this man has destroyed my life! He has destroyed the lives of my family and it's time the legal system did something about it! When I was 13 this man would not allow me to eat breakfast unless I read the Bible and prayed to God on a daily basis! He destroyed over 500 compact discs because they were not religious bands. I have come home on numerous occasions to find my bedroom completely ransacked and several personal items missing. This man kicked me out of the house in late October, 1997, with no coat, no shoes, nothing. He literally pushed me from my bedroom through the kitchen and entrance and out the door! (My mom was out of town.) Donald has not spoken a word to any of us kids for at least 9 months. If he ever does say anything, look out! I was kicked out again during Thanksgiving dinner, 2000. This time for wearing a "Pennywise" (punk band) T-shirt. When I was 13, I was wrestling with my cry-baby brother. I had my legs crossed around his stomach and was applying pressure. When he started crying, Donald grabbed me, threw me on the ground and did the same thing very hard, very many times. I cried and he continued. My best friends throughout high school were not allowed over. I was not allowed out of the house in junior high, as if that ever stopped a 14 year old kid. I saw Donald pull a 50 ft. garden hose through my brother Nathan's hands because he should have used a bucket to water the trees. When the end of the hose came through his fingers, there was blood everywhere! I remember getting spankings as a 14 year old, that I couldn't sit down for an hour! This is just a <u>hint</u> of the absolute hell that this man has put me and my family through. I, Kevin Parsons, swear the above stated is true. I will take whatever time off I need to remove this man from my life. Not only am I scared for myself, but for the well-being of my family. July 19, 2001— 10:30 pm. Kevin Parson.

Logan found Donald lying flat on the ground when he came home. Logan ran out to see if he was okay. Donald said no one cared and was shocked Logan even checked on him. Logan told me Donald talked about ending his life.

I came home that night—and there was Donald. I asked if he had not heard me that morning or didn't understand. I could tell he had put a few of his personal toiletries together and done a load of clothes, but he was still standing in front of me. I walked away from him shaking my head and asked what part of my words did he not comprehend? I walked upstairs to the bedroom and never came down the rest of the night.

The next morning, Nathan told me Donald had been upset with him that night. I asked why, as I had thought Donald was staying away from the kids.

Well, Nathan had been watching TV but was also talking on the phone to a friend who had called. This was a definite no-no. Donald took the remote away from Nathan and turned the volume way up. Nathan got up with the phone and started walking down the hall to continue talking. Donald disconnected the phone and came after Nathan. Donald pushed his finger on Nathan's chest and was right up in his face, almost touching nose to nose (according to Nathan). Nathan told him to back off and get lost (could have been more colorful from a 17-year-old). Nathan said he just wanted Donald to hit him. Nathan said he did everything in his power not to throw a punch at him. Finally Nathan told Donald he was calling the police and ran past him and took the car to a neighbor's. (I don't think Nathan called the police.)

The satellite was disconnected that night. No surprise for us. With Donald, it could be on for a day and off for two months, or on for two months and off again. Whatever suited Donald.

Donald left me a note on the kitchen cupboard the next morning and requested me to attend a communication class that he had gone to for a couple evenings. I left a note for him saying I'd love to attend, if he moved out—not for a day, not for a week, but indefinitely! Donald emailed me at work and stated he was out and the meeting was at 7 p.m. with the address.

When I came home from work, I noticed Donald had only taken some toiletries and a few pairs of pants and shirts. That was it! He still didn't get it! I wanted everything gone of his. Everything!

I thought, should I go to this communication class or not? I felt Donald hadn't totally moved out, but I decided to go anyway. The restraining order and divorce papers would be done soon and Donald would be served. So I attended this class with the doctor. It was an informative class and I thought I'd go back for more of his sessions.

A few days later, the judge granted the restraining order. Donald would be served!

CHAPTER TWENTY-THREE

DONALD WAS SERVED ON A FRIDAY MORNING. THE PERSON WHO served him said he was *not* happy. Donald emailed me, saying, "Thanks a lot for showing me how much you care!"

I never slept that night. I sobbed so long and hard and had so little sleep the past few months. I thought I'd have to admit myself to the hospital. I was cracking, emotionally drained!

The following week I still attended the evening classes with the doctor. I told the doctor what had been happening in our home and marriage. The doctor said we both needed professional help and that we should not live together. The doctor asked about the upcoming wedding for Logan.

Donald said he couldn't think about it and what good would it do if we're not speaking to each other. The doctor told Donald he was being childish and to put his feelings aside and that he really thought he should attend.

We started talking about the acreage and money issues and Donald said he didn't want to discuss it; it was too soon. The doctor got forceful and told him to smarten up and this couldn't wait and that these issues *did* need to be discussed. The doctor said if Donald and I couldn't settle the money issue within the next few days, not to bother making any appointments because he had no hope for us, no hope for the marriage, and no point in more appointments. He told Donald that if he couldn't even talk to me about something like this and make arrangements while we're apart on how to pay the bills, that we were in *big* trouble and there was no point in going forward.

Donald called me a few days later and we met in a restaurant. I refused to be alone with him anywhere. Donald asked what I thought of the doctor. Then Donald proceeded to tell me his impression of him.

I had quit my job a while earlier and accepted a new one that was offered to me. My new boss appreciated me and I was being noticed for my capabilities.

Donald felt the doctor had encouraged me to quit my job and accept the new one, and that the doctor was helping me with my self-esteem and to believe in myself. I no longer needed Donald and we now had a new problem! Well, so much for Donald seeing the doctor. All Donald saw now was that the doctor was the problem, because he encouraged me too much to be independent. Go figure! Because the doctor wasn't siding with Donald, he wrote him off.

The wedding day was drawing closer. Donald was sending me numerous emails, love letters, and poems. I wasn't sure whether Donald was going to appear at the wedding. I ended up asking a friend for a ride for Olivia and me so we could be there a day or two early. I left the old car for Kevin and Nathan and prayed they wouldn't have car trouble on the way. It was a 1,000-kilometer trip. Once Olivia and I arrived at the hotel, we were dependent on Logan to drive us around to help in any way we could. When Kevin and Nathan arrived, I used my old car to drive to the airport to pick up my parents and sister and her hubby. They just looked at me when I arrived with an old two-door to pick up four people. We managed.

Donald arrived and so did Donald's brother and family and his sister and her hubby.

The wedding was beautiful. After the reception, my parents needed a ride back to the hotel more than twenty minutes away. I told my sister to take the car and I'd find a ride, as I felt obligated to stay and help with the cleanup of the reception hall. I humbled myself and asked Donald for the ride. We never said one word the whole way back. When we got to the hotel, he said he would leave his door open for me! Seriously? That's what he read into giving me a ride back? I left early the next morning with the couple who had brought me, with no goodbyes to anyone.

Then it was back to work. Back to decisions about the acreage and where to live. Back to financial stress. And, back to more emails from Donald.

I tried so very hard to keep up the acreage, but I just couldn't. It wasn't the garden and the lawns and the watering, it was the mortgage payments, utilities, gas to town every day, etc. What would I do if we got snowed in? I looked for a place to rent, found one, and told Donald he could move back to the acreage once we got things moved out. Donald was living in the shop this whole time with no shower, no kitchen, no bedroom. Nathan and Olivia were beyond fabulous with helping me. Nathan rounded up some of his friends and lifted so much of the furniture and hauled it to town for me, using their trucks. I made trip after trip with the car to load boxes and more boxes. A few fabulous, unbelievable men from church showed up to move some bigger items the last day. I took the furniture and dishes I had before we got married.

Then I went to work to make the home on the acreage livable for Donald. I washed the house from top to bottom—cupboards, floors, walls, closets, bathrooms, carpets. I scrubbed and moved the patio set into the kitchen so Donald would have a table and chairs. I left numerous plates, bowls, silverware, pots, and pans. I left dishcloths and tea towels. I left a dresser and a double bed, which I made up with clean sheets, blankets, and pillows. I left towels and washcloths. I left a television and stereo and all his CDs. I left the fridge, stove, microwave, washer, and dryer. I left numerous items we had obtained since we got married: lawnmower tractor, bagger, rototiller and trailer, push lawnmower, gas trimmer, wheelbarrows, barbecue, satellite, treadmill, and yard tools.

I knew I couldn't afford the acreage and the workload. Donald chose not to keep it either. We sold it a year later. I asked for Donald's permission to go back to the acreage—back into the house one more time, to clean out anything I may have missed the year before and to be sure it was clean to hand over. I drove into the yard and fell apart. I couldn't believe all the work we had done to create this yard from prairie dirt and cactus to this: all the trees we planted, driveway, underground sprinklers and lawn, garden area, firepit, and then the mobile and attached garage with the three bedrooms above. I hated living in the city. I loved the country. I fell on the floor and sobbed and sobbed. I didn't think I would be able to pick myself up and leave. I did *not* want to give this up! I somehow crawled to the door...stood...walked to the car...and drove away. My dreams and work gone!

A year and a half was spent with unending emails, love letters from Donald, gifts from Donald, confrontations, accusations, and condemnations. I was told over and over I wasn't willing to work on the marriage, that I was unforgiving because with forgiveness comes reconciliation, that I made a commitment to love until death do us part. One of the letters I received from Donald before the divorce was final stated that he tried to be a father to my children, to instill some values in their lives, to push them to succeed, to bring some stability to their lives.

One of the last letters I received was to tell me he loved me. He had typed out numerous Bible verses. He told me he would still take me back and forgive me. *"Husbands, love your wives, just as Christ loved the church and gave himself up for her"* (Ephesians 5:25). Then he spoke of divorce. *"And if she divorces her husband and marries another man, she commits adultery"* (Mark 10:12). He went on to say again he forgave me and would continue to pray for me and that my relationship with God would be restored. He went on to say the church failed us in our earlier struggles and they were failing again by allowing me to live a life of sin.

Do you not know that the wicked will not inherit the kingdom of God? Do not be deceived: Neither the sexually immoral nor idolaters nor adulterers nor men who have sex with men...will inherit the kingdom of God. (1 Corinthians 6:9–10)

To the married I give this command (not I, but the Lord): A wife must not separate from her husband. But if she does, she must remain unmarried or else be reconciled to her husband. And a husband must not divorce his wife. (1 Corinthians 7:10–11)

He went on to say he was being blunt with me because my salvation was in jeopardy!

For Donald, the only form of forgiveness was reconciliation. Not true. I did forgive him, but I was not going to continue to be abused, nor allow my kids to be exposed to any more abuse. I do have a relationship with Jesus Christ. I have no doubt in my mind that I *am* going to Heaven! If I can't believe God can forgive me, then I have nothing to live for!

The divorce was granted a year and a half after Donald moved out.

The property wasn't settled for another year after that. In spite of everything that I/we paid off for Donald, he still didn't feel he owed me anything. I say "I" because for four years while we were married he only took a salary of $6,500 annually. When our first house sold, we gave $22,000 to his ex-wife for child support that he was behind. In total, we paid his ex-wife $56,000 while we were married. "I" made these payments. He fought me and never agreed to pay any of it, nor did he attend any court hearings in regards to it. I was the one who made all the arrangements with the courts. Then there were his two student loans that he refused to pay, which I made arrangements for and began paying— one for $4,600 and one for $10,000. Then when we sold the acreage we had to pay over $31,000 for Donald's business loan (which I was forced into signing a personal guarantee on the house) and $14,000 to our credit line. So Donald's debts were all paid—child support payments were done because his kids were old enough, student loans paid off, business loan paid off. How lucky could you be? I settled for $13,800! I asked for that particular amount because it was cash Donald took from the business, which I also had shares in.

PART III

Chapter Twenty-Four

DOES/CAN LIFE GO ON AFTER TWO DIVORCES AND SEXUAL, PHYSICAL, and mental abuse? I believe it can! Don't give up hope!

It's not easy, believe me. I spent many hours crying so hard I wondered if I would be able to get up for work, or cook meals for the kids. I pushed myself and pushed myself. I wouldn't give in. I was too stubborn.

My faith in God stood strong! I couldn't have made it without Him. My devotional life delved into more scripture searching for reassurance and love. I studied the Psalms and other books searching for comfort. In the book of Psalms, David was crying out to God to rescue him. In Psalm 30:5 it says, *"Weeping may stay for the night, but rejoicing comes in the morning."* It carries on in verse 11 where it says, *"You turned my wailing into dancing; you removed my sackcloth and clothed me with joy."* Psalm 94:19 says, *"When anxiety was great within me, your consolation brought me joy."* Deuteronomy 32:4 says, *"He is the Rock, his works are perfect, and all His ways are just."*

I started going out again with friends. Not often. A girlfriend and I would go dancing for a few hours on a weekend once in a while. It felt good to get out of the house again. I would dance with anyone who asked me—even though I'm not a very good dancer. We were usually home before midnight. One night I caught the eye of a gentleman whom I had watched dancing superbly with others. I went back to my girlfriend and said I wanted *that* man to ask me to dance.

Guess what? A few weeks later, that man asked me to dance. While we were dancing, he said he had wanted to ask me numerous times but was too scared. I told him I had been watching him, and wondered why he asked everyone else but me and honestly felt it was because I couldn't dance well. I also told him I was just an old-fashioned country girl and would never ask a gentleman to dance with me.

My girlfriend and I decided to go for coffee after dancing one night, and asked that gentleman—Jim Draper—if he would like to join us. Funny thing, though, another gentleman overheard us and asked if he could join us also. I didn't want to be rude and say no. The other gentleman had been looking for my attention for several months and it became quite amusing how he shoved his way into our coffee time, pushed himself in front of Jim to open the door for me and making sure he sat beside me once we were seated. We visited and joked and when we parted and when we were walking to our vehicle, Jim quietly asked me for my number. None of us had paper, though, so I told him where I worked in hopes we'd reconnect one day. I had mentioned that my birthday was the following day and I'd be spending it alone.

A few days later at work I was talking to my girlfriend and had mentioned it would be nice if Jim and I would meet again. Amazingly, when I hung up from talking to her, I had a message light flashing on my phone. When I listened to the message I could not believe my ears. It was Jim stumbling for words, wondering if he had the right person, requesting a call back. I did call. We met for coffee a few nights later and talked for hours and hours; in fact, we were the last ones out of the restaurant.

I learned that Jim was divorced and had been alone for fourteen years. He has three girls between each of my boys' ages. The oldest daughter was married with a baby. Jim grew up on a farm in the prairies, like me. We shared numerous things in common—mostly our love for the country! We continued meeting on weekends and danced together. He'd phone and we would visit for hours. I was not looking to get involved in another serious relationship, but the male companionship was great!

Several months later, Jim told me he was going to his dad's farm and wondered if I'd be interested in going with him. I wanted to so badly, but felt uncomfortable being alone with him and meeting his dad (Jim's mom had passed about a year prior). The day he was going to leave, I phoned and asked if I could join him. I had kind of made up my mind that I was going to get to know the parents first before I'd ever think of having a serious relationship again.

His Dad welcomed me with open arms. We visited and then Jim and I went walking in the yard. Jim gave me a pair of rubber boots and we traipsed through the pasture and mud and manure puddles and he showed me the different buildings on the farm. (I think Jim was quite shocked that I would get muddy and venture through the pasture and enjoy every minute of it!) We then went horseback riding.

Later, I peeled potatoes and helped with supper. After supper I saw Jim's dad whispering to him. Jim disappeared downstairs and came back with a keyboard and placed it on the table. Jim had been telling his dad a bit about me and had mentioned that I played the piano. Jim's mom used to play and she and Jim's dad would sing and were in the church and community choir. The keyboard had not been touched since she passed away. I was touched and nervous. Jim's dad dug out some music books and he and Jim sang hymns as I played and sang with them. Every once in a while, the men were quiet, tears rolling down their cheeks. I would continue singing, choking back my emotions, knowing they were sharing memories of Mom. I fell in love with Jim's dad that night. It felt so much like home. My dad and I used to sing together around the piano all the time. I felt warm inside and so welcome! What a feeling!

Jim and I continued seeing each other—not exclusively, though. I was not about to commit to one person and he knew it. I would still go out for meals, or go to hockey games or play racket ball with other male companions. Jim would come to church with me.

I hadn't change churches, because my kids were involved with the youth. Now, this became an event! Donald was still attending this church. Donald would come dressed in a suit, prim and proper, and would walk to the very front row. The service would begin and a few minutes later he would throw a deliberate look back and scan the congregation and if he spotted me with Jim, he would proceed to interrupt the service by standing and walking out. He caused a scene like this, Sunday after Sunday after Sunday.

For Valentine's Day, I was at work and one of the girls said I must go to the front of the office. I had a singing telegram from a male quartet, compliments from Jim, which the whole office enjoyed with me. The girls were so jealous. Jim was so romantic! He also booked a small plane to take us over the city and countryside. How was he going to top that?

About nine months after I met Jim, his second daughter was preparing for her wedding. I helped her with a few of her decorations, went to her shower, and Jim invited me to the wedding. That was the weekend I told him I loved him. He had told me a long time prior this.

We were engaged eight months later. Yes…I know what you're thinking. Is she crazy? She's actually going to try marriage again! Well, I wouldn't live with Jim outside marriage, and it was becoming too difficult to be apart, so yes, I chose to marry again! Olivia was graduating, so the kids were grown and leaving.

We were married in July. It's been more than thirteen fabulous years. I wouldn't trade them for anything! We've shared three of our children's weddings. We have twelve grandchildren and only one of those births happened when we weren't yet a couple. We've gone through the death of his dad and both of my parents. We also went through the death of his brother and my brother-in-law. We are still in love and guess what? NO ABUSE!

Someone once told me, "The trials that imprison you…need not limit God's work in you."

Life is not always fair…but God is always faithful!